THE POWER OF PRESSURE POINTS

The Most Common & Effective Martial Art Pressure Points

R. BARRY HARMON

First published by Dog Ear Publishing
4011 Vincennes Road
Indianapolis, IN 46268
www.dogearpublishing.net

ISBN: 978-145754-341-8

This book is printed on acid free paper.
Printed in the United States of America

CONTENTS

DISCLAIMER

This book is designed and intended to be used as an educational resource to inform the public about the dangers of using pressure points for striking and grabbing. The author, publisher, and all contributing parties do not take responsibility for any injuries, harm, or deaths resulting from anyone using the information in this book for any purpose other than educational purposes.

Pressure points for healing or martial art methods presented in this book are for academic purposes only and should not in any way be considered to take the place of a physician or a licensed medical professional or qualified martial art professional. Any injuries or illness, whether related to pressure points or any other reason, should be diagnosed and treated by a licensed physician.

A licensed physician should be consulted before engaging in any physical activity.

Never engage in martial art training without proper guidance and instruction from a qualified martial art teacher.

The information in this book is for educational purposes only.

DEDICATION

This book is dedicated to my mentor Grandmaster Suh, In Hyuk and my family who has supported me through all the ups and downs and the trials of life.

Kuk Sa Nim, In Hyuk Suh

Grandmaster In Hyuk Suh's proper title is Kuk Sa Nim. He has trained in Korean Martial Arts since early childhood. He coined the name Kuk Sool in 1958 and founded Kuk Sool Won™ (Association) in 1961. He is recognized by the Korean Government as a top authority on Korean traditional martial arts.

I am proud to say he is my mentor, and I'm humbled by his incredible amount and depth of knowledge.

NOTE TO READERS

"This Book introduces martial artists to the most effective and commonly used pressure points". R. Barry Harmon, License Acupuncturist, 9th Dahn Black Belt in the World Kuk Sool Association

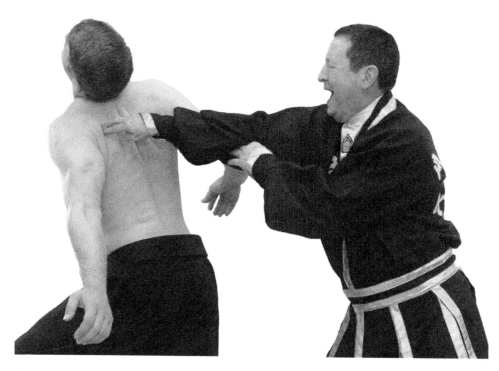

Any mistakes in the research or information in this book is the total and complete responsibility of the writer. In no way should any contributors be held responsible for the writer's opinions or mistakes.

This book is meant to help martial artists understand the power, use, and effectiveness of using pressure points for striking and grabbing purposes. This book will cover the most effective, the most common, and the most practical pressure points in martial arts; therefore, I will not cover every single pressure point that is used in martial art, acupuncture or healing. It will also include points or areas that are not regular pressure points but specific common areas that are used for martial art striking or grabbing.

I will not be discussing the anatomical or energetic effects of each point when struck but the effects of the strike on the pressure point. In other words, I explain what may happen to the individual when a particular pressure point is hit.

It was a very difficult decision to choose how much information to place in this book. The goal of this book is to include enough information to help the reader understand the pressure points and their possibilities. I have tried to avoid overwhelming the reader with more information than most martial artists are interested in studying. That said, I decided to include a little more information than most might be interested in concerning the theories of Ki, Um (Yin) -Yang, Five Elements, Channel theory, and pressure points. This information is specifically included for those martial artists that are interested in a more in-depth study.

ACKNOWLEDGEMENTS

I would like to express my heartfelt thanks to my family, Choon Ok, Emerald, Jada, and David, whose patience with me helped me complete writing this book. I would also like to thank my mentor, Grandmaster Suh, In Hyuk who taught me and stimulated my drive to learn more about pressure points and the more esoteric side of the martial arts. To Kuk Sool Won™ master Oh, Yi Kuen who first exposed me to the idea and use of pressure points through training in Kuk Sool. To Terry Heaps, a licensed acupuncturist and martial art master, who provided valuable information and input for the writing of this book. To Alex Skipp, whose help with pictures was invaluable. To C.J. and Lisa Farley for their help in reviewing this work. There are many others too numerous to name that have helped in the formation of this book, and to all those I offer my deepest respect and gratitude.

(Master Choon Ok and Master David relax for a minute between the painful photos for David.)

I would like to thank Choon Ok Harmon, David and Emerald Aue for holding still while having little dots placed on each pressure point and taking a picture. Thanks to Neil Woodbury for taking the color pictures in this book. Thanks to David Aue for preparing those pictures and placing them in this book.

A tremendous thanks to Nicole Jones for putting so much time and effort into editing this book.

INTRODUCTION

Martial Art Training: Some Facts

Longevity vs. Injury

Most martial artists are very short-term and technique-oriented, both in terms of training procedures and goals. That means that they practice a technique without regard to the consequences to their body, thereby shortening their training life and possibly causing lifelong physical problems.

Ever since Bruce Lee was introduced to the USA by Hollywood in the 1970's, there has been a lot of popular hype around him promoting an eclectic style and self supervised training. In truth, Bruce himself was a classically trained martial artist who did not take short cuts. He also received instruction from a Master Instructor.

However, movies and magazines of the time influenced many people who were interested in learning martial arts into thinking that it was better to "do your own thing" and the idea of traditional training became unglamorous. Instead of listening to a qualified Master Instructor who knows the way but takes more time, people will forgo the patience needed for healthy training and preferentially pick and choose whatever they want to work on, without knowledge and experience to guide them. Many fighters are able to gain remarkable fighting proficiency in a short period of time, but at what cost to their body and long term health? This is often the "sports" method of training.

Martial art training has two sides to it: the training for combat or fighting and the training for a long and healthy life. Those two sides of martial art *can* work together but are often at odds. Combat training is often severe, harsh, and unforgiving and can damage the body during the course of training. Health and long life training is often unrealistic and not effective for combat and fighting. In order for them to work together, it takes a very special and careful type of training.

Traditional martial art teachers proceed(ed) slowly, following certain laws of growth and development that were discovered and clarified over centuries and scores of generations. Training procedures and techniques may, and often do, affect the physical body and the body's energy flow in ways that only become apparent years later. This concept can be compared to the delayed effects of x-rays, food preservatives, environmental pollutants, etc.

Hand training

A type of training that many people practice is the striking of some object or surface to toughen or harden the striking appendage. There are two potential problems that are common side effects from this type of training. The first is that repeated micro-trauma results in obstruction to the flow of Ki, and the second is that blood may accumulate over time and cause a more serious obstruction. The hand is the most commonly trained part of the body for striking. *"Hit"* training, as it is often called, (sometimes called Iron Palm, Iron Wire Palm, or Steel Palm training), should only be practiced under the direct supervision of a qualified master instructor because of the possibility of serious short term or long-term injury. This type of training is based on the concept of doing a certain amount of controlled damage to the body under the assumption that in the repair process, the body's inherent feedback mechanism will modify flow and structure to cope with similar levels of stress in the future. In other words, it will make your hand harder and stronger to compensate for the extra stress of Hit training. However, It is especially important to immediately apply "Hit Medicine" to speed a healing resolution of all bruises and stress damage done in training in order to prevent any future problems.

Many years ago I met a young man whose specialty was breaking using his hands. He could break almost anything, but the cost to his body was great. He was only 31 years old, but his hands were always trembling. His nerves were damaged because his training methods were not for long-term health.

I know some masters that practiced Iron Palm, a technique that makes the hand very strong. These masters were in their 50s and still had no problems with their hands. Their hands were thicker than normal, but there were no negative effects from the training. They could break practically anything with their hand. This is the type of traditional training that I refer to; it takes longer but has no long-term ill effects.

Kicking

I met another black belt who loved kicking and had very fast and powerful kicks. He eventually had to stop kicking because his knees were hurting all the time, though he was in his 30s and very young for a martial artist. He also failed to follow the proper kicking methods that protect the knee joints. His training led to fast and powerful kicking very quickly, but his long-term health was not considered during his training. Many martial artists have come to me with knee pain but no knowledge of why their knee hurt. They said they could not kick anymore because it was too painful.

I watched them kick once and knew right away why their knee hurt: they were snapping their knee. It was a fast and powerful kick but terrible for the knee joint. That knee snap causes micro hyper-extension, which will build up over time and cause the knee to ache. If the practitioner continues to snap, the knee will ache worse and worse over time until the individual will not want to kick any more. I taught those same individuals a more traditional method of kicking, and within two months they could kick without pain.

On the opposite end of the scale I have known a number of martial artists in their 50s and older that have practiced correctly under the watchful eye of a qualified master instructor, and they had no ill effects from the training; rather, they had all the benefits such as power, speed, and good health.

Overtraining

Another problem that may arise from improper or excessive training is the overstressing of muscles, tendons, joints, ligaments and internal organs and over-fatiguing of the body's essential energy (Ki). Exercise stimulates the production of Ki and Blood. That is why it is important not to over train, not to train when excessively hungry, not to train when depleted by sex, not to train when over-tired, and not to train if you are high on alcohol or drugs. It takes Ki to make Ki. When Ki becomes depleted through lifestyle and diet, it is difficult to catalyze the production of more. It is very important to keep one's internal stores of Ki and Blood in good condition.

Traditional oriental medicine for martial arts

In traditional training under the tutelage of a qualified master instructor, the harmful side effects of intense martial arts training can be mitigated by the use of herbs, moxa, cupping, massage, acupressure/acupuncture, and specific training methods.

As stated previously, in order to prevent severe damage from hit training, herbal liniments are rubbed into the striking appendage to help promote the continuous smooth flow of Ki and blood. These types of liniments are commonly called "Hit Medicine." General Hit Medicine can be purchased from various companies, but there are many specific types that are often closely guarded secret herbal formulas. These formulas generally stimulate the superficial flow of Defensive Ki, activate the blood, and break up stagnation. They also tend to relax the tendons and ligaments, harden the bones, and disperse all coagulations.

In the past, martial artists also used herbal teas, decoctions and special foods on a regular basis to help keep their Ki and Blood from becoming depleted. Pressure point training was and still is a major method of helping the body to compensate for all types of training problems. Learning about and using pressure points can help individuals build, store, and circulate Ki and Blood for both good health and martial art power.

An excellent way to keep Ki and blood moving and in balance is regular preventative pressure point massage and regular massage. In ancient times the ascetics who spent their lives doing Ki Gong (Ki Breathing) often had trained assistants whose job was to provide them with daily therapeutic massage. It is also necessary for younger practitioners to practice more aerobic or vigorous exercises together with the internal training; because if more Ki is generated than can be circulated adequately, it will become obstructed internally and cause problems. Some of the problems caused by excessive Ki may be physical, and some may manifest themselves as mental oddness or even mental illness.

Meditation training

Meditation is a well-known technique for improving one's health as is verified by scientific study. Meditation is also a traditional martial art technique that is a very important part of training for both health and mental clarity in combat training. However, it is a technique that requires an experienced instructor.

I knew some people that were part of a group that practiced a type of meditation, but did not combine any physical activity with it. They just sat down in position and worked on letting their mind travel. They called it "astral travel" or "astral projection." They didn't know about Ki breathing to ground themselves or physical activity to balance out the meditation, so many of that group became very odd mentally, the more that they practiced.

I asked my mentor about that, and he said it was a phenomenon which occurred from improper practice. My mentor said that sometimes people went into the mountains to meditate, and, due to incorrect technique, they would descend from the mountain claiming they were god or some other mental malfunction. When people are not physically trained and mentally centered, every time that they "astral traveled" a miniscule part of their minds or consciousness became scattered or didn't return so over time and repetition they became mentally imbalanced due to improper Ki flow. I witnessed that oddness first hand.

Joint Health

Joint alignment is another way we can assist Ki flow. Proper alignment allows for maximum Ki flow through the body and puts less wear and tear on the body's joints. Additionally, to maintain healthy joints for long life we must learn not to snap the joints, especially the knee and elbow joints. Snapping motions in the air cause micro hyper-extension that damages the joint over time. To prevent this hyper-extension, especially when kicking or punching, we must use the focusing technique. This technique allows one to prevent any joint damage and trains the Ki to flow more directly into the target. (However, detailed descriptions of the methods and techniques used to protect the body when training is not part of this book. This will be the focus of another book, and it will have more specific information concerning this subject).

Another way in which we can develop and maintain a healthy flow of Ki is by correct martial art training itself. Under the tutelage of a qualified Master Instructor, martial arts students are able to feel and see the effects of careful, healthy manipulation of joints, and proper use of pressure points. In practice, martial artists have the opportunity to strike, kick, grab pressure points and twist the joints of training partners, and vice versa, which helps keep joints supple and Ki flowing smoothly. Also, proper training can help the body to maintain a healthy, youthful look. Looking and moving approximately 10 to 20 years younger is not an uncommon trait for martial artists that follow these methods.

Conclusion

Knowing about Ki is essential to becoming a better martial artist or fighter. Muscle power is amplified through Ki training. Muscle power even at its maximum level is short lived and weaker compared to a body energized and developed with Ki. It is ideal to have healthy strong muscles, tendons, joints, and ligaments, with complete body alignment and powerful Ki development, all working together to give the body the maximum potential, power, and longevity possible.

Kuk Sa Nim, In Hyuk Suh says that most people's life cycle is: *"We are born, we grow up, we grow old, we get sick, and we die."* Kuk Sa Nim says that our goal as Kuk Sool martial artists is this: *"We are born, we grow up, we grow old, and we die."* Kuk Sa Nim says that our goal as Kuk Sool martial artists is to leave out the *"get sick"* part.

$$\textbf{\textit{"We are born, we grow up, we grow old, }} \sout{\textbf{\textit{we get sick,}}} \textbf{\textit{ and we die."}}$$
"In Hyuk Suh"

KI AND THE UM – YANG CONNECTION

This information comes directly from my mentor, Grandmaster In Hyuk Suh. Grandmaster Suh is considered to be one of the world's foremost authorities on the development and practice of Ki in martial arts.

As martial artist we are always working on power and precision. The development and use of Ki is very important for both power and precision. The following is a very brief explanation by Grandmaster Suh of this development.

Internal training revolves around Ki. Often described as a mysterious inner energy force, Ki is the source of internal strength and is tied closely to breathing and blood circulation. In order to become proficient, the martial artist must develop his/her Ki through meditation and special, often secret, breathing exercises.

Ki can be classified into two types, "prenatal" (before birth) and "postnatal" (after birth). There are three pressure points in a straight vertical line directly below the naval that represents the area of prenatal Ki. Before birth and at birth this Ki is fully developed. However, as a child grows up and experiences stress and develops bad habits, he/she loses the development of Ki at these points. Yet this form of Ki is what determines internal strength or power.

Postnatal Ki centers are located at three vertical pressure points directly above the navel. This Ki develops after birth and is the source of external strength. Postnatal Ki is easily replenished by eating nutritious foods and by getting enough sleep. Postnatal Ki is the external power and energy that most martial artists spend their time developing.

The two points that are used to combine external and internal Ki strengths are located directly above the navel (Conception 9, Soo Boon) and directly below the navel (Conception 7, Um Kyo). From the combination of those two points comes a circular pattern that extends into the other Ki pressure points, while at the same time, blending them together. This blending of Ki is often referred to as the Um and Yang (Yin and Yang in Chinese) combination. In this view, the postnatal Ki represents Yang while the prenatal Ki has the characteristics of the more passive Um aspect of the energy.

If a martial artist develops only postnatal Ki, he will have just the strength potential of one person. If he/she concentrates only on his/her prenatal (internal) Ki, then he/she will have developed and stored that Ki. As a stored commodity; it won't be of any use to him/her in the martial arts. The object is to combine both prenatal and postnatal Ki into a pattern that provides one person with the strength potential of seven. To do this is the true potential and goal of martial art Ki training. This is the ultimate Kuk Sool Won™ technique power for which we strive. More detailed information about "Ki is on page 202 and "Um (yin)-Yang" is on page 204.

Three Postnatal and Three
Prenatal Ki Pressure Points

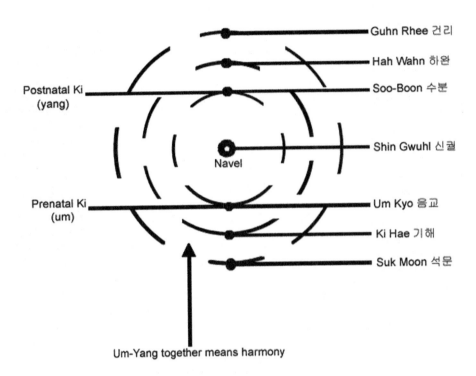

THE FIVE PHASES/ ELEMENTS IN APPLICATION

This provides a description of the "Five Phase / Element Theory" as it relates to:

1. **The Hyung (Form) principals of Kuk Sool Won™:**

   EYES which are bright and powerful like sunshine and relate to **"FIRE"** which is powerful, fast, bright, and full of excitement.

   MIND should be clear, focused, and unwavering and relates to **"METAL"** which is precise, disciplined, and discerning.

   BODY should be supple, soft, and low and relates to **"WATER"** which is fluid, adaptive, and seeks the lowest point.

   FEET should be deliberate, balanced, and slow compared to hands and relates to **"EARTH"** which is overall absorbing, stable, and balanced.

   HANDS should be fast, expanding, and covering and relates to **"WOOD"** which expands, grows, and is always reaching.

2. **Technique training principals of Kuk Sool Won™: "You-Won-Hwa"**

   You: 유: The best translation is supple. Sometimes it's translated as soft which tends to present an idea of weakness in the western mind which is not correct.

   Won: 원: This translates best as circular.

   Hwa: 화: This translates best as Harmony or Harmonizing.

   The "Five Phases" as they relate to the technique principals.

   Wood expands to learn new technique. (Won)
   Fire promotes active practice and training.
   Earth absorbs and integrates the skill set into the mind and body. (Hwa)
   Metal facilitates a more precise practice and training.
   Water promotes the ability to flow smoothly and adapt theory to application. (You)

3. The controlling cycle of five phases as it relates to sparring:

Opponent weakness	Defeated by	Control cycle
(Fire) Light, quick but no stamina	Fluid adaptive movement and wearing them out	Water defeats Fire
(Metal) Straight, strong, and predictable	Quick use of multiple techniques	Fire defeats Metal
(Wood) Tall, stiff and inflexible	Low spin kick that is attacking their base	Metal defeats Wood
(Earth) Short, stable and exposed from the top	Attack to the head and upper areas of the body	Wood defeats Earth
(Water) Bloated, Heavy, fluid and slower	Absorb, adapt and redirect the attacks	Earth defeats Water

4. Personality types and student development:

This next section will talk about the promoting and controlling interaction as applied to personality types and student development. It may help the instructor understand themselves and his/her students better so the instructor may teach better.

Fire: The fire type personality student is full of energy and enthusiasm but is often not consistent in their training. They tend to overdo it and then not show up for weeks or months. They have a problem with control.

The instruction to help counter this type is that the instructor should give enough technique to keep them interested (Wood), while encouraging a more balanced and consistent training schedule (Earth).

Earth: The earth type personality student is balanced in training, always at the Dojang, loyal and participates in the school activities. Other students and instructors tend to depend on this student, so much so that there is a danger of the student getting overwhelmed and stuck or frustrated.

The instruction to counter this type is that the instructor needs to support the student's enthusiasm (fire) but allow or encourage the student to take some free time away from the Dojang or use meditation to expand their horizons (wood).

Metal: The metal type personality student is somewhat rigid in their thinking, seeing even a slight variation in technique as a completely new technique. They tend to be disciplined but get frustrated if there is a lot of variation or too much is taught all at once. They are usually sticklers for etiquette and although they like people, they tend to be viewed as cold or tough. Typically these students are hard core and love precision, sometimes so much so that it can hinder their training.

The instruction to counter this type of personality is that the instructor should teach in small balanced patterns (earth) and encourage the student towards openness and to be more adaptive (water).

Water: The water type personality student is typically very easy going but generally has a problem with motivation. This student usually doesn't like sparring and will do as little practice as possible to get through the syllabus.

The instruction to counter this type of personality should encourage discipline (metal) and encourage the student to take private lessons, extra classes, and participate in group demos (wood).

Wood: The wood type personality student is always searching for the new technique. They usually learn very well and can be seen as a "natural". However, this personality type gets bored easily and goes off in search of new knowledge when they perceive they are not learning.

The instruction to counter this type of personality should encourage to student to discover the variation within the techniques they already know (water) and thus generate their continued interest (fire).

Being able to recognize these phases and understand their interaction will benefit your development in Kuk Sool Won™ or any other martial art. Keep in mind that we are all a mixture of these five phases, and tendencies may change with various factors mentioned at the beginning of this section. Knowledge is power, and study brings knowledge. Don't just train absentmindedly; study and continue to learn forever. Grandmaster Suh leads by example and says that we should never stop studying or training no matter our age or situation. He continues to do both to this day.

More detailed information about the "Five Phases (Elements)" is on page 206.

"TRADITIONAL BODY MEASUREMENTS"

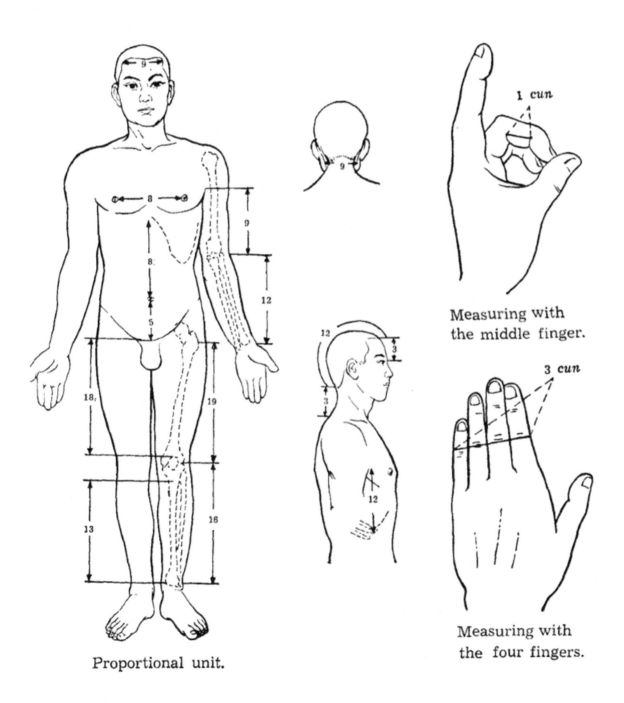

Proportional unit.

Measuring with the middle finger.

Measuring with the four fingers.

These measurements were and still are used to locate pressure points accurately.

POINT AND BODY LOCATION MEASUREMENTS

Location of pressure points is not measured in absolute units. They are measured in relative, proportional units of the given individual. The proportional units are called **"Chon"** (Korean) (**"Cun"** in Chinese, pronounced seun) and (**"Sun"** in Japanese). Since it is a proportional measurement system it is equally applicable to adult or children as well as to thin or obese subjects. Units can be measured with the length or breath of the individuals' fingers.

*The width of the thumb at the middle joint is measured as one unit or "cun". Also the distance between the ends of the creases of the inter-phalangeal (middle knuckle) joint of the middle fingers at their widest point is 1 cun.

*The width of the index and middle fingers together are measured as 1.5 cun.

*The length of the index finger from the second joint to the tip is considered to be two cun.

*The width of four fingers excluding the thumb, held close together, and measured at the distal joint, is three cun.

In the profession of acupuncture it is generally accepted that pressure (acupuncture) points are approximately one millimeter in diameter.

Considering that points are so small in size and very often protected by muscles, it is vitally important that the location of each point be as accurate as possible in order to be as effective possible. If a point is not located accurately it is likely to have no effect at all or at least a greatly diminished effect upon attempted usage.

Throughout the profession of Acupuncture the term "Cun" and its unit of measurement for locating all pressure points is the most common method used. In this book I will continue to use the common term "Cun" when referring to the measurements of body and pressure point distances.

LOCATING PRESSURE POINTS

This guide is intended to help martial artists be sure of the locations they've been taught, and to help them understand both the healthful effects of the kind of pressure point manipulation that occurs in the course of regular, healthy training, and the potential dangerous effects of "over-stimulation and damage." Because pressure points can help or hurt an individual it is extremely important that the martial artist learns correctly from a qualified Master Instructor. Also there are specific methods and techniques for striking, kicking, and grabbing pressure points in different locations of the body. Having a qualified Master Instructor teach these methods is a must for correct and safe training.

COMMON ANATOMICAL TERMS

Proximal – Closer to the center of the body

Distal – Further from the center of the body

Superficial – Closer to the skin

Deep – Further from the skin

Dorsal – Towards the back of the body

Ventral – Towards the front of the body

Pronate – Turn the palms down or rotate the feet inward

Supinate – Turn the palms up or rotate the feet outward

Abduction – To move away from the middle of the body

Adduction – To move toward the middle of the body

*These two words differ by only one letter. The second letter, "d" or "b" makes all the difference and can cause confusion.

Extension – To straighten out a joint

Flexion – To bend a joint

Dorsiflexion – To bend the foot upward at the ankle

Plantarflexion – To bend the foot downward at the ankle

Cranial – Closer to the head

Caudal – Closer to the buttocks

Foramen – A hole or opening

Fossa – A flat surface or a depression

Lumen – The opening of a tube (like the center of the windpipe or a blood vessel)

Prominence – An area that protrudes or sticks out

Tubercle – A bump

OUTLINE OF STUDY EXPLANATION

*The Channel (Meridian): is listed first followed by the individual point number the Korean name and the Asian (Chinese) character.

*Location: The standard location of each point.

*Location Note: Any special information about the point location.

*Special Note about the Name: This note says something specific about the name of the pressure point listed.

---

*STRIKE: The most common directions to strike, grab or use the point.

*OBSERVED EFFECTS: The observed effects of the strike to that point. This refers to the effects of that point that I have personally observed.

*KNOWN EFFECTS: The known effects of striking that point. This refers to the effects that I know occur because a credible source I know has observed the effects first hand.

*THEORETICAL EFFECTS: The theoretical effects of striking that point. Effects that are theoretically possible though haven't been observed by me or heard by me through first-hand credible sources

*Special Note for Application: This note tells something about the point that is very important concerning information or emergency treatment using the point noted.

---

*Explanation: This explains something specific and interesting about the point.

*Primary Actions and Functions of the point. This explains on an energetic level something important about the point.

*Korean: The Korean name in English, the English translation and meaning, and the Korean writing (Han Gul).

*Chinese: The Chinese name in English, the English translation and meaning, and the Chinese character.

*Japanese: Japanese name in English. Japanese use the same character as Chinese.

*Special Note: Any special note or information for that particular point.

Additional Information:

Pressure points are very small (~1mm) therefore actually striking a pressure point is quite difficult. It is common to use the hand or foot to strike pressure points and because the hand or foot is so much larger than a pressure point it is very common to hit more than one point at the same time. In doing so it can not only cause the specific effect of striking that pressure point but the surrounding area may be damaged as well. In the section of "effects of striking" some of the descriptions may include a description of damage of the surrounding area that is normal with a non-pressure point strike.

THE LUNG CHANNEL

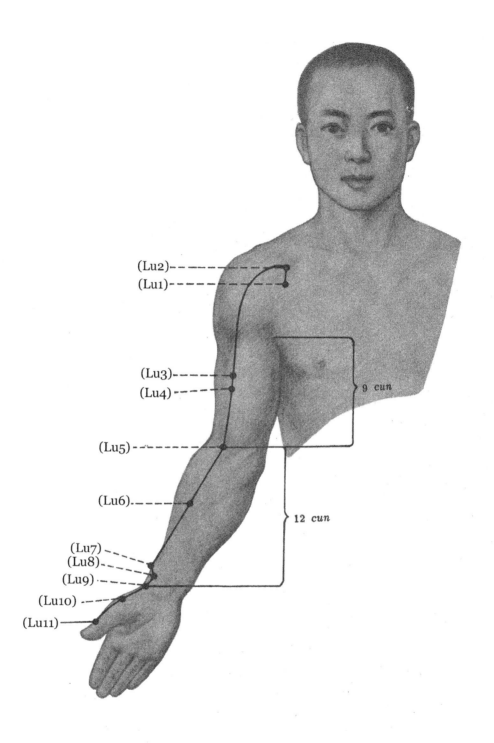

(Lu2)
(Lu1)
(Lu3)
(Lu4)
(Lu5)
(Lu6)
(Lu7)
(Lu8)
(Lu9)
(Lu10)
(Lu11)

9 cun

12 cun

The Lung Channel

Superficial pathway and measurement on the body

For Lung channel flow and functions see page 182.

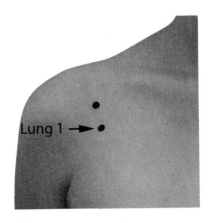

Lung (Lu 1): 중부 : 中府

Location: At the level of the 1ˢᵗ intercostal space (ICS), 6 cun lateral to the midline, 1 cun inferior to the fossa clavicularis (Lu 2).

Striking: Straight in, slightly upward or slightly inwards towards the middle of the body.

Observed effects of the Strike: Local pain, local tingling and numbness, bruising, inability to use the shoulder, breathing problems, and dislocated shoulder or AC joint, or broken bones.

Known effects: Pain spread over the entire chest region, which can cause difficult breathing.

Theoretical effects: Ki drainage that can spread. May cause fullness and distention in the abdomen. May cause diarrhea. May cause wasting syndrome due to lack of the body's ability to convert food into its appropriate Ki energy. May cause knockout.

Explanation: This point on the chest is the meeting place of the Lung and Spleen meridian. The vital energy stored in the chest is the compound of respiratory gas and the essence of water and grain. The formation of the essence depends on the functional activities and the vital energy of the spleen and stomach in the Middle Burner.

Primary Actions and Functions: Regulates Lung Ki. Stimulates the Lung Ki to descend. Clears and diffuses the upper burner and courses the Lung Ki.

Korean: Joong Boo - Middle Palace, Residence, or Treasury: 중부

Chinese: Zhong Fu: Zhong = middle, inside the chest, middle Burner. Fu = storehouse. 中府

Japanese: Chufu

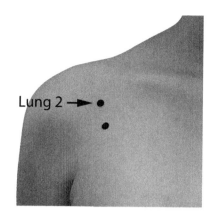

Lung (Lu 2): 운문 : 雲門

Location: 6 cun from the midline Superior to the coracoid process of the scapula in the Fossa clavicularis. In the depression below the acromial extremity of the clavicle, 1 cun above Lung 1.

Striking: Straight in or upwards. Slightly inwards towards the middle of the body.

Observed effects of the Strike: Local or radiating pain, tingling and numbness in shoulder, bruising, momentary paralysis, dislocated shoulder or AC joint, broken bones, breathing problems.

Known effects: Can cause considerable internal damage without much external sign. Long lasting paralysis. This point may cause a knockout.

Theoretical effects: This point may cause death due to massive Ki drainage.

Explanation: This point on the chest is where the respiratory gas and essence formed from water and grain rise up and fall down. The network of small vessels in the lung is compared to clouds in the sky.

Primary Actions and Functions: Disperses fullness from the chest. Stimulates the descending and disseminating actions of Lung Ki. Clears Lung heat. Dispels agitation and fullness.

Korean: Oon Moon: Cloud Gate or Door: 운문

Chinese: Yun Men: Yun = Cloud, referring to the compound of respiratory gas and essence formed from water and grain and the network of all the small vessels in the lung. Men = Gate. 雲門

Japanese: Unmon

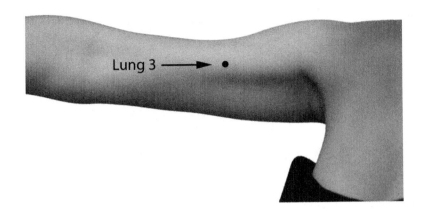

Lung (Lu 3): 천부 : 天府

Location: On the medial aspect of the upper arm, 3 cun below the end of the axillary fold, on the radial side of the muscle biceps brachii. In the depression between the lateral borders of the Biceps brachii muscle and the shaft of the humerus bone 6 cun superior to Lung 5.

Location Note: This is a point on each of the arms at about the same level as the nipples of man, so it is just in touch with the nipple when the arms are folded.

Striking: Straight into the point is the most effective direction.

Observed effects of the Strike: An effect like an electrical shock that may travel up or down the arm, bruising, and momentary paralysis of the arm. This point causes "dead arm" (temporary paralysis of the arm).

Known effects: This point may cause instant vertigo or long lasting paralysis of the arm.

Theoretical effects: This point is a "window of the sky" point and can cause serious imbalance between the Ki of the lower and upper parts of the body. May cause emotional problems with confusion and loss of memory.

Special Note for Application: This point can be used to stop a bleeding nose by applying finger pressure to this point on both arms.

Explanation: It is the name for the two Breast. This point belongs to the Lung Channel and is responsible for the storage of respiratory gas.

Primary Actions and Functions: Disseminates Lung Ki and dissipates harmful influences. Calms the corporeal soul. Clears Lung heat, cools the blood and regulates Lung Ki.

Korean: Chun Boo: Heavenly Palace or Residence (Celestial Storehouse): 천부

Chinese: Tian Fu: Tian = Heaven, referring to atmosphere, the upper part of the human body. Fu = Storehouse. 天府

Japanese: Tenpu

Lung (Lu 5): 척택 : 尺澤

Location: This point is on the cubital crease, in the depression on the radial side of the tendon of the muscle biceps brachii. This point is usually located with the elbow slightly flexed.

Striking: Straight into the point. This point is also effective for grabbing techniques.

Observed effects of the Strike: Pain, bruising, numbness and tingling that travels down to the hand. Temporary numbness and loss of power in elbow area down to the hand.

Known effects: This point can cause knockout if struck with enough power.

Theoretical effects: This point can damage the entire system by causing a major Ki imbalance in the upper body. This imbalance will cause a complete loss of power. It is possible to cause brain damage striking this point with enough power.

Explanation: This point is located in the depression at the elbow, in the medical classics the elbow is often referred to as "chi" (a unit of measurement about a foot long), and the wrist as "cun" (one tenth of a chi, that is, a little longer than an inch).

Primary Actions and Functions: Clears lung heat, descends rebellious Ki, regulates the water passages, activates the channel, relaxes the sinews and alleviates pain. Discharges Lung fire, down bears counter flow Ki and clears upper burner heat.

Korean: Chuck Taek: Cubit Marsh: 척택

Chinese: Chi Ze: Chi = A unit of length (about a foot), the ulna is called the "chi bone" because it is about a foot long. Ze = Depression (indentation). 尺澤

Japanese: Shakutaku:

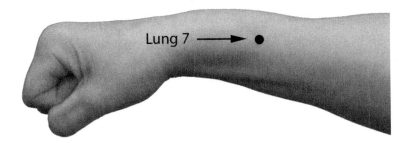

Lung (Lu 7): 열결 : 列缺

Location: 1.5 cun above the wrist crease in the depression below the radial stolid, in the cleft between the tendons of the medial brachioradialis and medial abductor pollicis longus muscle.

Striking: Straight into the point from the side of the arm or from the inside of the wrist at the radial pulse area. There is a special grabbing technique that is very effective with this point.

Observed effects of strike: Pain, bruising, numbness. Causing an electrical sensation traveling up or down the arm. Creating enough pain to the point of tears flowing and mental confusion. Temporary paralysis of hand and wrist.

Known effects: It's possible to cause major imbalance between Um and Yang of the Lung and Large Intestine causing stomach or intestine or lung problems.

Theoretical effects: May create grief with sobbing and may interfere with the ability to learn physical things that can get worse over time.

Explanation: The ancient Chinese people called lightning "Lieque". The point is located in the crevice above the styloid process of the radius. The propagation of sensation caused by striking or puncturing at this point is usually rapid like lightning.

Primary Actions and Functions: Stimulates the descending and dispersing of Lung Ki. Circulates the body's defensive Ki, expels exterior wind and opens and regulates the conception vessel. Benefits the bladder and opens water passages, opens the nose, and communicates with the Large Intestine. Benefits the head and nape. Diffuses the Lung and dispels cold, courses the channels and frees the connecting vessels. Activates the channel and alleviates pain.

Korean: Yuhl Gyuhl: Broken Sequence: 열결

Chinese: Lie Que: Lie = Split open. Que = gap or crevice. 列缺

Japanese: Rekketsu

Special Note: The name of this point "Broken Sequence" is an ancient term for lightning. We may understand the meaning of "broken sequence" in three ways. The first is the electrical sensation that can be generated when striking or needling this point.

The second is the ability of Lung 7 to clear heaviness and oppression of the chest in the way a lightning storm clears the sky.

The third is the sudden fork this channel takes at Lung 7.

THE LARGE INTESTINE CHANNEL

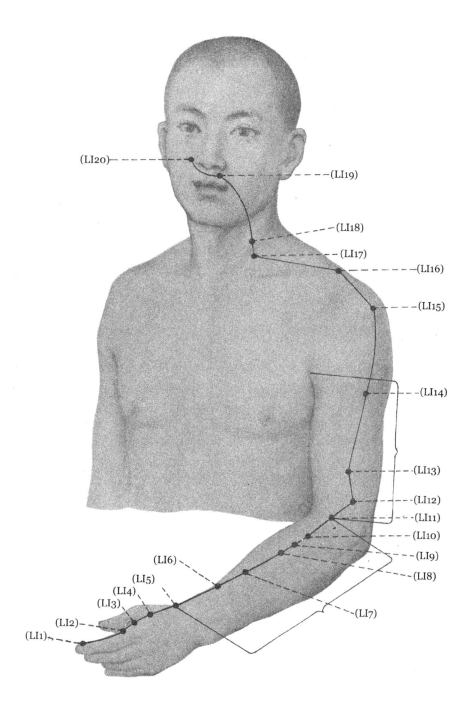

The Large Intestine Channel

Superficial pathway and measurement on the body

For Large Intestine channel flow and functions see page 183.

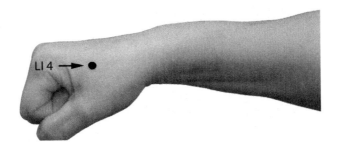

Large Intestine (LI 4): 합곡 : 合谷

Location: On the dorsum of the hand, between the first and second metacarpal bones, at the midpoint of the second metacarpal bone and close to its radial border.

Striking: Straight in to point or slightly up towards the metacarpal bone. Gripping is more common with this point.

Observed effects of strike: Pain, bruising, numbness in hand. It is possible to cause enough pain to weaken the knees and confuse the individual.

Known effects: It is possible to cause enough pain locally that total confusion in the brain occurs.

Theoretical effects: Can promote contractions in the lower musculature.

Special Note for Application: This point is contraindicated in pregnancy. Do not press strike or message this point during pregnancy. It has the strong action of inducing labor.

Explanation: This point is between the metacarpal bones. When the thumb and the index finger are put together, a small hill is formed, and when they part, a valley-like depression is formed. The interface of two adjacent muscles is also called a valley.

Primary Actions and Functions: Stimulates the dispersing function of the Lungs. Removes obstructions from the channel, tonifies Ki and consolidates the exterior. This point also harmonizes ascending and descending functions. Regulates the defensive Ki and adjusts sweating. Activates the channel and stops pain. Frees the channels and quickens the connecting vessels, clears and discharges Lung heat and frees gastrointestinal down-bearing. This point relieves pain and quiets the spirit.

Korean: Hahp Gohk: Joining Valley: 합곡

Chinese: He Gu: He = Put together or close. Gu = Valley. 合谷

Japanese: Gokoku

Special Note: Large Intestine 4 is considered to be (physically) the second largest pressure point in the body.

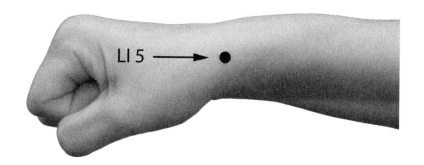

Large Intestine (LI 5): 양계 : 陽谿

Location: On the radial side of the wrist, in the center of the hollow formed by the tendons of extensor pollicis longus and brevis.

Striking: Straight in to the point. Gripping is more common with this point.

Observed effects of strike: Pain, bruising, numbness in wrist and hand.

Known effects: Create enough pain to cause a person to collapse to the ground.

Theoretical effects: It is possible to damage and dislocate the wrist joint.

Explanation: The point is located in the stream-like depression of the lateral side of the wrist joint.

Primary Actions and Functions: Clears heat and stops pain. Calms the spirit and benefits the wrist joint. Dispels wind and drains fire. Dissipates bright yang pathogenic heat.

Korean: Yang Gyea: Yang Stream or Ravine: 양계

Chinese: Yang Xi: Yang = Referring to Yang channels and back of hand. Xi = Stream. 陽谿

Japanese: Yokei

Special Note: This point was and is known as the "Anatomical Snuffbox."

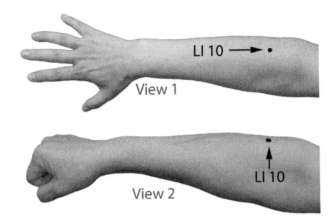

Large Intestine (LI 10): (수) 삼리 : 手三里

Location: On the radial side of the forearm, 2 cun distal to Large Intestine 11 on the line connecting Large Intestine 11 and Large Intestine 5. Locate with the elbow flexed and with the radial side of the arm upwards.

Striking: Straight in to the point or slightly upwards towards the elbow or slightly downwards towards the hand. Gripping is common with this point.

Observed effects of strike: Pain, bruising, an electrical sensation that may travel up or down the arm, temporary paralysis of the arm. This point can make the knees buckle.

Known effects: May cause nausea, Ki imbalance in upper body, or diarrhea.

Theoretical effects: May cause shock strong enough to knock out or possibly even stop the heart due to severe shock to the system.

Explanation: This point is about three cun from the olecranon. The inside of the human body is divided into three parts, upper, middle and lower. This point has an effect on all the three inside parts.

Primary Actions and Functions: Regulates Ki and blood, activates the channel and alleviates pain. Tonifies Ki and removes obstructions from the channel. Harmonizes the intestines and stomach. Dispels wind and frees connecting vessels. Invigorate and regulate the circulation of Ki and Blood in the upper limb as a whole.

Korean: Soo Sahm Nee: Arm Three Miles or Measures: (수) 삼리

Chinese: Shou San Li: Shou = Upper limb. San = Three. Li = a unit of length or inside. 手三里

Japanese: Te no sanri

Special Note: Ancient martial artist were known to use this point to re-energize the arm from exhaustion after extreme arm training, especially extreme weapons training or combat.

Large Intestine (LI 11): 곡지 : 曲池

Location: When the elbow is flexed to 90 degrees, in the depression between the lateral end of the transverse cubital crease and the lateral epicondyle of the humerus.

Striking: Straight in to the point. Gripping and striking is common with this point.

Observed effects of strike: Pain, bruising, numbness in elbow, damaged elbow joint. This point can force the elbow to bend when the arm is straight.

Known effects: May cause diarrhea.

Theoretical effects: May cause nausea and vomiting.

Explanation: This point is located in the pool-like depression at the external end of the elbow crease when the elbow is flexed.

Primary Actions and Functions: Clears heat and cools the blood, alleviates itching, Regulates Ki and blood, Activates the channel and alleviates pain. Harmonizes Ki and blood, Eliminate pathogenic heat and disinhibits the joints.

Korean: Gohk Jee: Pool at the Crook; Crooked Pond or Pool at the Bend: 곡지

Chinese: Qu Chi: Qu = Crook or flex. Chi = Pool. 曲池

Japanese: Kyokuchi

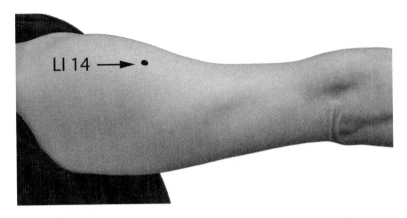

Large Intestine (LI 14): 비뇌 : 臂臑

Location: On the lateral side of the upper arm, in the visible and tender depression formed between the distal insertion of the deltoid muscle and the brachialis muscle, approximately three fifths of the distance along the line drawn between Large intestine 11 and Large Intestine 15 and 7 cun above Large Intestine 11.

Striking: Straight in to point. This point is more commonly used as a point to press.

Observed effects of strike: Pain, bruising, numbness and inability to use the arm.

Known effects: Broken bone from pressing technique or striking.

Theoretical effects: Ki damage to the entire body causing extreme weakness and emotional problems.

Explanation: This point is on the upper arm below the shoulder.

Primary Actions and Functions: Activates the channel and alleviates pain, Regulates Ki and dissipates phlegm nodules and Sharpens eyesight. Frees the channels and connecting vessels and relieves pain. Clears channels and vision.

Korean: Bee Noe: Upper Arm or Arm and Scapula: 비뇌

Chinese: Bi Nao: Bi = upper limb or upper arm. Nao = Muscles below the shoulder. 臂臑

Japanese: Hiju

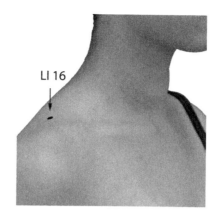

Large Intestine (LI 16): 거골 : 巨骨

Location: In the depression medial to the acromion process and between the lateral end of the clavicle and the scapular spine.

Striking: Straight into the point for the maximum effect.

Striking Note: This point is usually hidden somewhat between the bones and is more difficult to strike directly. Usually the entire area is hit often breaking the AC joint.

Observed effects of strike: Pain, Bruising, dislocated AC joint.

Known effects: This point can knock out the person. Broken bones locally.

Theoretical effects: Ki drainage from the body causing weakness. Broken bone could penetrate the lung causing a pneumothorax or hole in the lung.

Explanation: This point is called "Big Bone" because the point is near the big clavicle bone.

Primary Actions and Functions: Activates the channel, alleviates pain and benefits the shoulder joint. Regulates Ki and blood and dissipates phlegm nodules. Courses and quickens the connecting vessels and disinhibits the joints.

Korean: Kuh Gohl: Great Bone: 거골

Chinese: Ju Gu: Ju = Big or Great. Gu = Bone. 巨骨

Japanese: Kokotsu

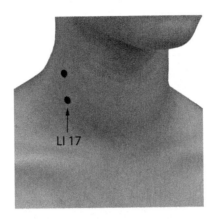

Large Intestine (LI 17): 천정 : 天鼎

Location: On the lateral side of the neck, on the posterior border of the sternocleidomastoid muscle, 1 cun inferior to Large Intestine 18.

Striking: Any angle will work on this point especially up, downward, or straight in. Due to location striking up is very difficult.

Observed effects of strike: Pain, bruising, brain fog or confusion (sometimes called "out on the feet"), knock out.

Known effects: Unconsciousness.

Theoretical effects: Possible coma or death.

Explanation: This point is used to mean the head and neck. The point is on the neck near the throat; the important gate for inhaling the atmosphere of the heaven.

Primary Actions and Functions: Benefits the throat and voice. Clears Lung Ki, Disinhibits the throat.

Korean: Chun Jung: Heaven's Tripod or Celestial Vessel: 천정

Chinese: Tian Ding: Tian = Heaven referring to atmosphere or the upper part of the human body. Ding: An ancient cooking vessel or treasured object having two loop handles and three legs. 天鼎

Japanese: Tentei

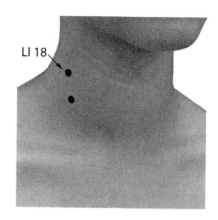

Large Intestine (LI 18): 부돌 : 扶突

Location: On the lateral side of the neck, level with the tip of the Laryngeal Prominence (Adam's apple) between the two muscle heads of the sternocleidomastoid muscle.

Striking: Any angle will work on this point including anterior or posterior directions but up, downward or straight in work especially well.

.**Observed effects of strike:** Pain, bruising, brain fog or confusion (out on your feet), or knockout.

Known effects: May cause a blocked feeling in the throat or unconsciousness.

Theoretical effects: May affect the emotions severely, or cause coma or death.

Explanation: This point is on the neck sustaining the head, which is the biggest projection of the body.

Primary Actions and Functions: Benefits the throat and voice and alleviates cough and wheezing. Regulates Ki and blood and disinhibits the throat.

Korean: Boo Dohl: Support the Prominence: 부돌

Chinese: Fu Tu: Fu = To Sustain and support. Tu = Projection. 扶突

Japanese: Hutotsu

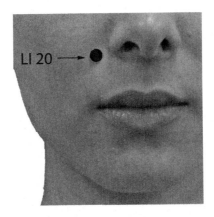

Large Intestine (LI 20): 영향 : 迎香

Location: In the nasolabial groove, at the level of the midpoint of the lateral border of ala nasi.

> **Striking:** Straight in to the point is most effective. A special grabbing technique may be used on this point.
>
> **Observed effects of strike:** Pain, bruising, tearing of eyes, weakness in the knees, knockout.
>
> **Known effects:** Broken facial bones.
>
> **Theoretical effects:** Unconsciousness or coma.

Explanation: Pressing this point enables the stuffy nose to identify odors, to welcome and meet fragrance.

Primary Actions and Functions: Opens the nasal passages, expels wind and clears heat. Unlocks the nose, dissipates wind pathogen and clears Ki fire.

Korean: Young Hyang: Welcome Fragrance: 영향

Chinese: Ying Xiang: Ying = Welcome or meet. Xiang = Fragrance. 迎香

Japanese: Geiko

THE STOMACH CHANNEL

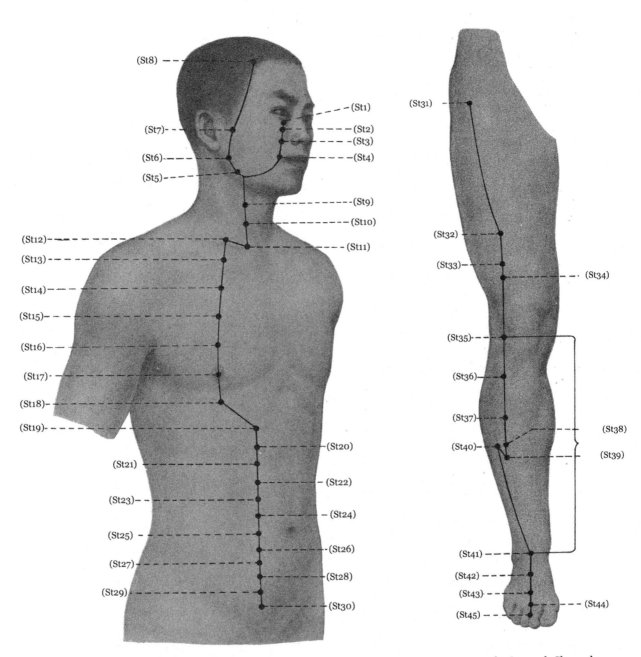

The Stomach Channel

The Stomach Channel

Superficial pathway and measurement on the body

For Stomach channel flow and functions see page 183.

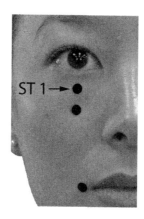

Stomach (St 1): 승읍 : 承泣

Location: With the eyes staring directly forward, this point is located directly below the pupil between the eyeball and the infraorbital ridge.

Striking: Straight in to the point.

Observed effects of strike: Pain, bruising (black eye), swelling, impaired vision or lack of vision, and eye damage, knockout.

Known effects: Extreme nausea. Broken eye socket. Unconsciousness and coma. Can pop the eye out of socket.

Theoretical effects: Drainage of Ki especially from the upper body. May also affect the liver. Possible death.

Explanation: This point is at the middle of the lower rim of the eye socket. That is the place for tears.

Primary Actions and Functions: Brighten the eyes, Stops lacrimation, and Expels wind. Dispels wind, brightens the eyes, stops lacrimation.

Korean: Seung Eup: Container of Tears: 승읍

Chinese: Cheng Qi: Cheng = Receive. Qi = Tear. 承泣

Japanese: Shokyu

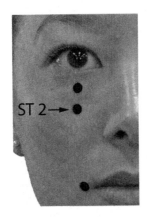

Stomach (St 2): 사백 : 四白

Location: With the eyes looking directly forwards the point is located 1 cun directly below the pupil, in the depression at the infraorbital foramen.

Striking: Straight in to the point or downward angle.

Observed effects of strike: Pain, bruising (black eye), swelling, impaired vision or lack of vision and eye damage, weekness in the knees, knockout.

Known effects: Dizziness, broken eye socket, unconsciousness.

Theoretical effects: Downward drainage of Ki, nerve damage, possible coma.

Explanation: This point is used to treat eye diseases and to enable the eye to see all around clearly.

Primary Actions and Functions: Eliminates wind, clears heat and brightens the eyes. Quickens the connecting vessels, soothe the sinews and relieves pain.

Korean: Sah Baek: Four Whites: 사백

Chinese: Si Bai: Si = Four, referring to all directions, all around. Bai = White, referring to bright or clear. 四白

Japanese: Shihaku

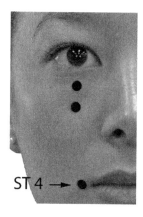

Stomach (St 4): 지창 : 地倉

Location: 0.4 cun lateral to the corner of the mouth. Note: This point lies in the continuation of the naso-labial groove; ask the patient to smile if the groove is not visible.

Striking: Straight in to the point. This point is also commonly used for gripping and pressing.

Observed effects of strike: Pain and confusion. Bruising and Swelling. Chipped teeth.

Known effects: Broken or completely knocked out teeth.

Theoretical effects: May generate enough shock to the system to cause knockout.

Explanation: This point is beside the corner of the mouth. The mouth is compared to a part of the granary.

Primary Actions and Functions: Eliminates wind from the face, Activates the channel and alleviates pain. Dispels wind and frees Ki stagnation.

Korean: Jee Chang: Earth Granary: 지창

Chinese: Di Cang: Di = Land, soil, or the grain produced on the land. Cang = Granary. 地倉

Japanese: Chiso

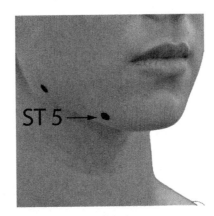

Stomach (St 5): 대영 : 大迎

Location: Directly anterior to the angle of the jaw, in a depression at the anterior border of the masseter muscle.

Location Note: To help locate this point clench the jaw before locating, also you may feel the pulsation of the facial artery in the groove like depression appearing when the cheek is bulged. Also you may measure from the center of the eye straight down to the jaw and locate the point.

Striking: Straight in to the point gets the best results but any angle will work.

Observed effects of strike: Pain, bruising, swelling, dizziness and knockout.

Known effects: Broken jaw, broken teeth.

Theoretical effects: This point can affect the Ki to the brain causing concentration problems.

Special Note for Application: In times past this point was known as the "Glass Jaw" point because striking it directly with minimal power would cause knockout.

Explanation: This point name is the ancient name for the mandible. It receives the grand and rich atmosphere to nourish the body.

Primary Actions and Functions: Eliminates wind and reduces swelling. Quickens the connecting vessels.

Korean: Dae Young: Big Welcome or Great Reception: 대영

Chinese: Da Ying: Da = The atmosphere or grand and rich. Ying = Welcome or meet. 大迎

Japanese: Daigei

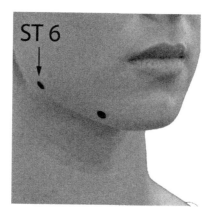

Stomach (St 6): 협거 : 頰車

Location: The width of a middle finger anterior and superior to the corner of the jaw; when the jaw is firmly clenched at the prominence of the masseter muscle where it attaches. There is a slight depression at the point location.

Striking: Any angle will work but straight into the point is best.

Observed effects of strike: Pain, bruising, swelling, dizziness, dislocated jaw and knockout.

Known effects: Nausea or broken jaw.

Theoretical effects. May cause brain concussion from shock of impact, possible memory loss, or emotional instability.

Explanation: Joints of the jaw or movable like a wheel.

Primary Actions and Functions: Expels wind, removes obstructions from the channel. Opens the jaw and frees the connecting vessels, dispels wind and regulates the Ki.

Korean: Hyup Guh: Jaw Bone or Jaw Chariot or Jaw Vehicle: 협거

Chinese: Jia Che: Jia = Cheek or maxilla. Che = Mandible or wheel. 頰車

Japanese: Kyosha

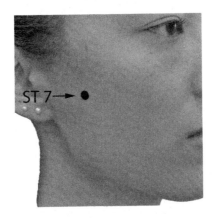

Stomach (St 7): 하관 : 下關

Location: In the lower border of the zygomatic arch, in the depression anterior to the condyloid process of the mandible.

Striking: This point is most effective with a strike straight in to the point; however, any angle will cause strong effects.

Observed effects of strike: Pain, bruising, swelling, dislocated jaw, out on your feet.

Known effects: Knockout, unconsciousness.

Theoretical effects: Ki drainage, ear problems caused from a strong strike.

Explanation: This point is below the joint of the jaw and zygomatic arch.

Primary Actions and Functions: Activates and removes obstructions from the channel. Benefits the ears, jaw and teeth. Alleviates pain, opens the portals and sharpens hearing.

Korean: Ha Gwan: Lower Gate or Hinge: or Below the Joint: 하관

Chinese: Xia Guan: Xia = Lower or below. Guan = Joint. 下關

Japanese: Gekan

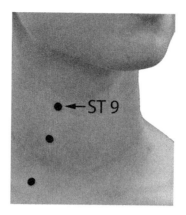

Stomach (St 9): 인영 : 人迎

Location: Level with the tip of the Adam's apple, 1.5 cun lateral to the upper edge of the laryngeal prominence, where the pulsation of the common carotid artery is palpable, on the anterior border of muscle sternocleidomastoideus (SCM), next to the carotid artery.

Striking: In to the point at an angle towards the spine will give the maximum results but striking at any angle will have strong effects with this point.

Observed effects of strike: Pain, bruising, swelling, difficulty breathing, and choking and gagging.

Known effects: Choking and gagging strong enough to incapacitate the individual. Knockout.

Theoretical effects: Unconsciousness, coma, death due to severe disruptions of Ki and blood to the head. Also, damage to the artery may cause death.

Explanation: The arteries on two sides of the laryngeal prominence are called "In Young" in Korean (Renying in Chinese). It receives pneuma (air) from the sky and the ground and from the internal organs as well and then nourishes the body with this pneuma (air).

Primary Actions and Functions: Regulates Ki, Benefits the throat, relieves swellings and alleviates pain. Opens the channels and connecting vessels, Clears heat and calms dyspnea.

Korean: In Young: Man's Welcome (or Prognosis) or Person's Outcome: 인영

Chinese: Ren Ying: Ren = Human body or life. Ying = Welcome, receive or meet. 人迎

Japanese: Jingei

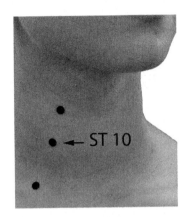

Stomach (St 10): 수돌 : 水突

Location: On the neck, at the anterior border of the sternocleidomastoid muscle, midway between "In Young" St. 9 and "Ki Sah" St. 11.

Location Note: To identify the anterior border of the muscle, ask the individual to turn their head away from the side to be located, while you apply resistance at the chin.

Striking: Straight in to the point from the front at an angle of about 45 degrees is the best angle to strike, but any angle will have a strong effect.

Observed effects of strike: Pain, bruising, swelling, difficulty breathing, choking and gagging.

Known effects: Choking and gagging strong enough to incapacitate the individual. Knockout.

Theoretical effects: Unconsciousness, coma, death due to severe disruptions of Ki and blood to the head. Also, damage to the artery may cause death.

Explanation: This point is located in the place where the essence of water and grain flushes out.

Primary Actions and Functions: Benefits the throat and neck. Descends Lung Ki.

Korean: Soo Dohl: Water Prominence or Fountain: 수돌

Chinese: Shui Tu: Shui = The essence of water and grain. Tu = Hole made through chiseling, cutting or digging. 水突

Japanese: Suitotsu

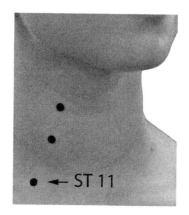

Stomach (St 11): 기사 : 氣舍

Location: At the root of the neck, on the upper edge of the medial end of the clavicle (collar bone), directly below "Soo Dohl" St. 10. In the depression between the sternal and clavicular heads of the sternocleidomastoid muscle.

Location Note: Feeling the sternal and clavicular heads is made easier if the individual turns their head away from the side to be felt, while you apply resistance at the chin.

Striking: Downward into the "Clavicle Notch". This point is more commonly used as a point to press into.

Observed effects of strike: Pain, bruising, swelling, and can make the knees and legs weak, legs collasping.

Known effects: Strong enough pain to cause a person to pass out.

Theoretical effects: Damaging effect on the upper end of the lung. This point may stop the heart causing death.

Special Note for Application: When the heart stops, some claim that this point may also restart the heart by applying very strong stimulation directly on the point.

Explanation: This point is near the throat, the dwelling place and the passage for respiratory gas.

Primary Actions and Functions: Benefits the throat and neck and relieves breathing difficulty. Descends the Ki.

Korean: Ki Sah: Ki's Residence or Ki Abode: 기사

Chinese: Qi She: Qi = Respiratory gas. She = Dwelling or reservoir. 氣舍

Japanese: Kisha

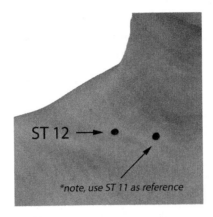

ST 12 → ●   ●

*note, use ST 11 as reference

Stomach (St 12): 결분 : 缺盆

Location: In the center of the supraclavicular fossa (behind the middle of the collar bone), 4 cun lateral to the ventral midline.

Striking: Downward straight into the point. This point is more commonly used as a point to press into by hooking the clavicle (collar bone).

Observed effects of strike: Pain, bruising, enough pain to make the legs weak and person collapse, broken clavicle (collar bone).

Known effects: Will drain the fight away from the individual and incapacitate them.

Theoretical effects: It's possible to damage the sub-clavian vessels. It's also possible to damage the upper part of the lung with a very strong strike.

Special Note for Application: The "Systematic Classic of Acupuncture and Moxibustion", says do not use this point during pregnancy. Do not press strike or message this point during pregnancy. It has the possibility of inducing spontaneous abortion.

Explanation: This name means a basin without a cover. It is an ancient term in anatomy. The point is located in the basin-like depression in the center of the supraclavicular fossa.

Primary Actions and Functios: Descends Lung Ki, Regulates Ki and Blood. Activates the channel and alleviates pain.

Korean: Kyuhl Boon: Empty Basin: 결분

Chinese: Que Pen: Que = Vacancy: Pen = Basin: 缺盆

Japanese: Ketsubon

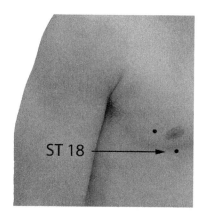

Stomach (St 18): 유근 : 乳根

Location: On the chest directly below the nipple on the lower border of the breast, in the fifth intercostal space, 4 cun lateral to the midline.

Location Note: In males the nipple lies in the fourth intercostal (rib) space so this point is one space lower in the fifth. In females this point lies at the root of the breast, below the breast tissue itself. In females the nipple should not be used as a reference point because the nipple location may vary considerably.

Striking: Straight in to the point. This point is far more dangerous to strike on the left side of the body toward the valves of the heart.

Observed effects of strike: Pain, wind knocked out, bruised ribs, cracked ribs.

Known effects: Knockout

Theoretical effects: A strike on the left side may send enough shock into the heart to cause heart fibulation (heart flutters and can't pump blood properly), causing heart attack and death.

Explanation: This point is so named because the point is at the base of the breast.

Primary Actions and Functions: Regulates the stomach Ki and breast lactation, Dispels stagnation. Quickens the blood and transforms depression.

Korean: You Guen: Breast Root: 유근

Chinese: Ru Gen: Ru = Breast. Gen = Base. 乳根

Japanese: Nyukon

Special Note: According to the "Ode of Xi-Hong" this point may be used to promote and hasten pregnancy labor even though it's not contraindicated in pregnancy.

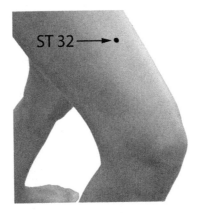

Stomach (St 32): 복토 : 伏兔

Location: On the line connecting the anterior superior iliac spine and lateral border of the patella (knee cap), 6 cun above the lateral top of the knee cap in the middle of the belly of the rectus femoris muscle.

Striking: Straight in to the point.

Observed effects of strike: Pain, bruising, swelling and temporary leg paralysis.

Known effects: May damage the blood vessels severely causing the leg to be completely unusable for weeks or months.

Theoretical effects: May shock the system enough to cause a knockout.

Explanation: This point is above the upper margin of the patella, where the muscles look like a prostrate rabbit.

Primary Actions and Functions: Removes obstructions from the channel and alleviates pain. Warms the channels and dissipates cold.

Korean: Bohk Toe: Crouching Rabbit or Hidden Rabbit: 복토

Chinese: Fu Tu: Fu = Prone or prostrate. Tu = Hare or rabbit. 伏兔

Japanese: Fukuto

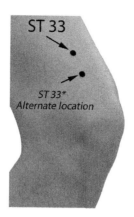

Stomach (St 33): 음시 : 阴市

Location: On the thigh, on a line drawn between the anterior superior iliac spine and the superior lateral corner of the patella, in a depression 3 cun proximal to this corner. In the depression three cun above the laterosuperior border of the patella. (About 3 cun above the outside corner of the knee cap.)

Alternate Location for this Point: In traditional Korean martial arts this point is often located approximately 1.5 cun above the lateral (outside) corner of the knee cap.

Striking: Straight in to this point gives the best result however, striking this point at any angle will give some results.

Observed effects of strike: Great pain in the leg causing difficulty in walking. Bruising and swelling in local area.

Known effects of strike: Can send an electrical shock up or down the leg.

Theoretical effects: May cause Ki drainage from the leg or a Ki rush to the head which may cause confusion. A powerful strike to this point may cause a blackout.

Explanation: This point is directly above the outside edge of the knee cap. It is used in some martial arts, Kuk Sool in particular to train for toe kicking. It can help the practitioner prevent straitening the leg too far when they preform a toe kick.

Primary Actions and Functions: Activates the channel and alleviates pain. Dispels the wind and dissipates cold. Disinhibits the joints.

Korean: Um Shi: Um =Um (yin) energy: Shi = Market: 음시

Chinese: Yin Fu: Yin = yin energy: Fu = ancient term for the short clothing covering pudenda. Yin Fu is so called because the point is at about the lower margin of the short clothing. 阴市

Japanese: Inshi

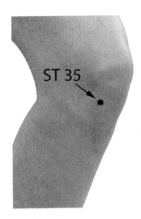

Stomach (St 35): 독비 : 犊鼻

Location: On the Knee, in the hollow formed when the knee is flexed, immediately below the patella (knee cap) and lateral to the patellar ligament.

Striking: Straight in to the point.

Observed effects of strike: Pain, swelling, bruising. Loss of energy and inability to walk.

Known effects: Torn patella tendon, dislocated patella (knee cap), broken knee joint.

Theoretical effects: May damage the body's Ki causing loss of power and tiredness.

Explanation: This point is in the depression at the lateral side below the patella ligament, which looks like the nose of a calf.

Primary Actions and Functions: Relieves swelling and stops pain. Activates the channel and quickens the connecting vessels.

Korean: Dohk Bee: Calf's Nose or Eyes of the Knee: 독비

Chinese: Du Bi: Du = Calf. Bi = Nose. 犊鼻

Japanese: Tokubi

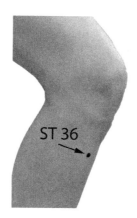

Stomach (St 36): (족) 삼리 : 足三里

Location: 3 cun below Stomach 35, one finger breadth (middle finger) from the anterior border of the tibia.

> **Striking:** Straight in to the point, however striking at an angle will give some results.
>
> **Observed effects of strike:** Will cause great pain and deaden the leg so one cannot walk. This point will hurt for a long time and may continue to get worse if untreated.
>
> **Known effects:** Great physical leg damage. Will also break the knee with a very strong strike.
>
> **Theoretical effects:** This point can cause major problems for the internal organs. This point will also damage the spleen and will continue to get worse to the point of incapacitating the individual if left untreated.

Explanation: This point is three cun below the Stomach 35. This point has an effect on all the three inside parts of the body. The upper, middle and lower parts of the body.

Primary Actions and Functions: Strengthens the body, Tonifies the Ki and blood, brightens the eyes, raises the Yang, and regulates the nutritive and defensive Ki and the intestines. Regulates the central Ki. Frees and regulates the Ki and Blood of the channels (meridians). Dispels illness and prevents disease.

Korean: Johk Sahm Nee (Ri or Lee): Leg Three Miles or Leg Three Measures: (족) 삼리: Johk is the leg. Sahm mean three. Lee (Ri) is the ancient measurement for a mile. It's approximately one third of a modern mile.

Chinese: Zu San Li: Zu = The lower limb or foot. San = Three. Li = A unit of length referring to "cun". 足三里

Japanese: Ashi no Sanri

Special Note: Ancient martial artist were said to have used this point to help them continue to kick or march even after they were exhausted. They messaged or treated this point to revive the leg for kicking or marching another three Lee (miles). This point is considered to be (physically) the largest pressure point in the entire body.

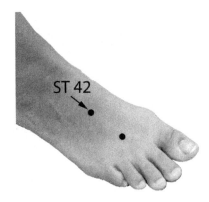

Stomach (St 42): 충양 : 沖陽

Location: On the dome of the instep of the foot between the second and third metatarsal bones and the cuneiform bone, where the pulsation of the dorsal artery of the foot is palpable.

Striking: Straight down onto the point will have the greatest effect. Angle strikes will have some effect. Also, pressing into this point with a knuckle or object is a common technique.

Observed effects of strike: Great pain and swelling. Can cause a person to collapse to the ground in pain. Can cause momentary confusion due to pain and may feel an electrical type of shock travel up the leg.

Known effects: Broken foot bones. Numbness of the foot and ankle.

Theoretical effects. May cause great Ki loss. Also this point can cause nerve damage as well as damage to the foot artery (dorsalis pedis artery).

Explanation: This point is at the highest place on the back of the foot, above Liver 3.

Primary Actions and Functions: Calms the spirit (mind), activates the channel and alleviates pain. Stabilizes the spirit, harmonizes the Stomach and transforms damp.

Korean: Choong Yang: Rushing (surging) Yang (yang energy): 충양

Chinese: Chong Yang: Chong = communications hub or impulse. Yang = back of the foot. 沖陽

Japanese: Shoyo

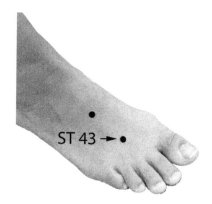

Stomach (St 43): 함곡: 陷谷

Location: In the depression distal to the junction of the second and third metatarsal bones. Another description says in the proximal corner of the second metatarso-phalangeal joint, between the second and third metatarsal bones.

Striking: Straight down into the point will have the greatest effect. Angle strikes will have some effect: the greater the angle the less the effect. Pressing this point is common with a knuckle or object and can produce a strong effect.

Observed effects of strike: Great pain, bruising and swelling. Can cause a person to collapse to the ground if strong enough pressure is applied. May cause momentary confusion due to great pain. May cause loss of balance and prevent the individual from standing on that foot. This point can also cause broken foot bones.

Known effects: Previous damage can cause long-term foot problems such as undefined pain.

Theoretical effects: May cause significant loss of energy in the foot and leg. If not properly treated it may cause rheumatism later on.

Explanation: The meridian energy travels down into the valley. The sunken ground can hold water. So the name sunken valley infers that this point can treat edema.

Primary Actions and Functions: Activates the channel and promotes urination. Eliminates wind and heat. Removes obstruction from the channel.

Functions: Eliminates wind from the channels. Regulates and harmonizes the Stomach and Intestines. Regulates the Spleen and dispels edema.

Korean: Hahm Kok: Sunken Valley: Hahm (sunken) Kok (valley): 함곡

Chinese: Xiang Gu: Xiang = pitfall, pit, sink in, or from a higher place to a lower place. Gu = valley. 陷谷

Japanese: Kankoku

THE SPLEEN CHANNEL

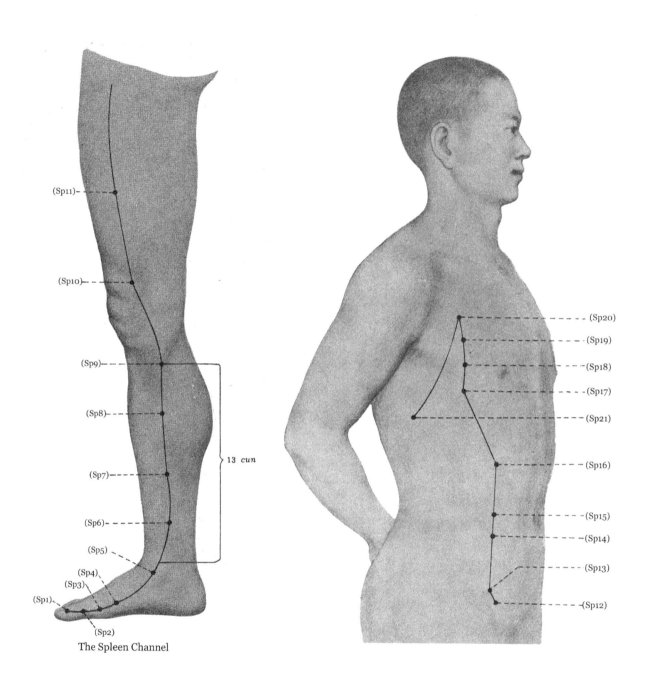

The Spleen Channel

The Spleen Channel

Superficial pathway and measurement on the body

For Spleen channel flow and functions see page 184.

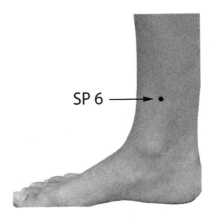

SP 6 →

Spleen (Sp 6): 삼음교 : 三陰交

Location: 3 cun directly above the tip of the medial malleolus (inside ankle bone), posterior (behind) to the medial border of the tibia (the big leg bone).

Striking: Straight in to the point. Strikes at an angle will lessen the effect greatly. This point is also effective with the proper grip and applying pressure to the point.

Observed effects of strike: Great pain, numbing the leg and foot, unable to stand on that leg, and mental confusion.

Known effects: Possible broken bone and lower leg paralysis.

Theoretical effects: A downward or drooping feeling in the lower part of the body. Strong nausea may be felt. Also, sudden or spontaneous defecation may occur.

Special Note for Application: This point is contraindicated during pregnancy. Do not press strike or message this point during pregnancy. It has the strong action or inducing labor.

Explanation: This point is the place where the Spleen Channel of the foot, the Kidney Channel of the Foot and the Liver Channel of the foot meet.

Primary Actions and Functions: Strengthens the Spleen, Tonifies the Kidneys, Nourishes the blood and Um, Promotes the function of the Liver and smooth flow of Liver Ki, Stops pain and Calms the mind. Frees Ki stagnation, Resolves and expels dampness.

Korean: Sahm Um Kyo: Three Um Intersection or Junction: 사음교

Chinese: San Yin Jiao: San = three. Yin = Yin channel of the foot. Jiao = Meet. 三陰交

Japanese: Saninko

Special Note: All three Um (Yin) channels of the leg meet at this point.

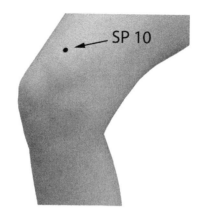

Spleen (Sp 10): 혈해 : 血海

Location: With the knee flexed, 2 cun proximal to the medial superior border of the patella on the bulge of the vastus medialis muscle. Or when facing the person and their knee is flexed, cup your right palm to the left knee, with the thumb on the medial side and the other four fingers fully extended and directed proximally, (up the leg) and the thumb forming an angle of 45 degrees with the index finger. The point is where the tip of your thumb rests.

Striking: Straight in to the point is most effective, but 90-degree angles will still give a strong effect. Gripping and pressure techniques are also commonly use on this point. The greater the striking angle the less effective the strike.

Observed effects of strike: Great pain, inability to walk, leg paralysis.

Known effects: This point gives a strong shock throughout the system. Can cause knockout.

Theoretical effects: Causes the blood to become "reckless," which opens the system to pathogens (illness). A strong strike may interfere with proper blood circulation and cause the body's defense to become weak.

Explanation: This point is the sea or reservoir of blood. It has the function of regulating blood, keeping it circulating normally.

Primary Actions and Functions: Cools the blood, removes stasis of blood and tonifies the blood. Alleviates nausea, regulates and clears the blood.

Korean: Hyul Hae: Sea of Blood: 혈해

Chinese: Xue Hai: Xue = Blood. Hai = Sea or reservoir. 血海

Japanese: Kekkai

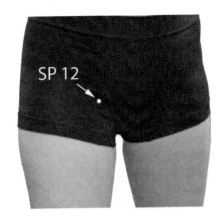

Spleen (Sp 12): 충문 : 沖門

Location: On the lateral end of the groin, 3.5 cun lateral to the central point of the upper edge of the pubic symphyses, lateral to the A. iliaca externa.

Location Note: Palpate (feel) to locate the pulsation of the femoral artery, just over one handbreadth lateral to the midline, at the level of the upper border of the pubic symphyses. Spleen 12 is in the depression immediately lateral (outside) to this pulsation.

Striking: Straight in to the point. Pressing this point is as common as striking.

Observed effects of strike: Extreme pain, numbing of the hip area and causing hip and leg paralysis so you are unable to walk.

Known effects: So much injury in that area the person cannot walk for a day to a couple of weeks or longer.

Theoretical effects: Possible dislocation of the hip joint, knocking the ball right out of its socket. Possible damage to the femoral artery and or the femoral nerve. Ligaments and tendons may also be damaged. This point can cause permanent injury or death.

Explanation: This point is on the lower abdomen, from where upward waves of distension gas begin, causing diseases

Primary Actions and Functions: Invigorates blood, regulates Ki and alleviates pain. Tonifies Yin, Clears heat, Drains damp and regulates urination.

Korean: Chong Moon: Rushing (Surging) Gate (Door) or Pouring Door: 충문

Chinese: Chong Men: Chong = Rush up. Men = Gate. 沖門

Japanese: Shomon

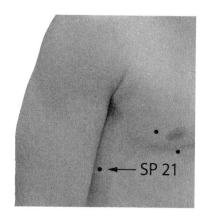

Spleen (Sp 21): 대포 : 大包

Location: On the lateral side of the chest and on the mid axillary line (mid armpit line), 6 cun below the axilla (arm pit) in the 6th ICS (inter-costal space). Some sources say it's in the 7th ICS.

Striking: Straight in to the point. The more open the ribs are the more effect a strike will have. The more closed the ribs are the more protected this point is.

Observed effects of strike: Pain, untreated the pain may get worse and last a long time, temporary paralysis of movement, wind knocked out, cracked ribs, total knockout.

Known effects: Lungs or liver may be punctured if ribs are broken inward too far.

Theoretical effects: Spleen damage, possible severe contraction of lungs causing suffocation, coma, possible death.

Explanation: The vast human body is embraced by the congenital (prenatal) vital energy and the postnatal acquired vital energy. The spleen is the middle earth, surrounded by the other four internal organs. This forms a great surround.

Primary Actions and Functions: Regulates Ki and Blood, Moves blood in the blood connecting channels. Firms the sinews and joints, Benefits the lateral costal region.

Korean: Dae Po: Great (Big) Wrapping (Enveloping) or General Control: 대포

Chinese: Da Bao: Da = Big or human being. Bao = To include, embrace or surround. 大包

Japanese: Daiho

THE HEART CHANNEL

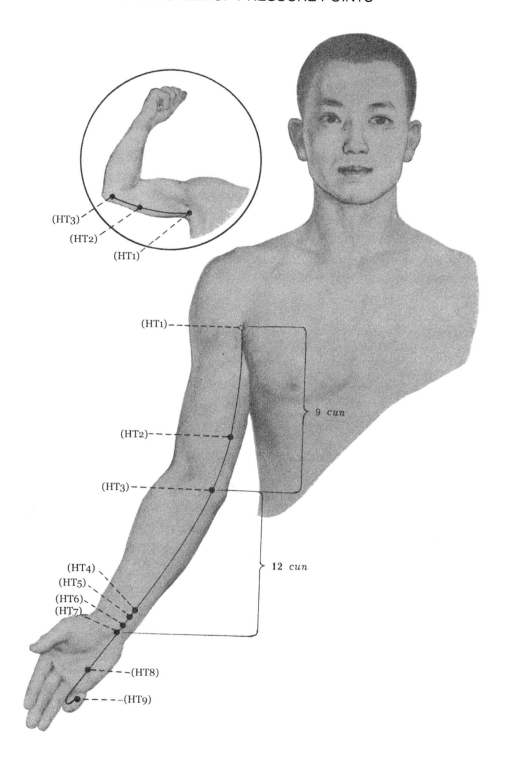

The Heart Channel

Superficial pathway and measurement on the body

For Heart channel flow and functions see page 185.

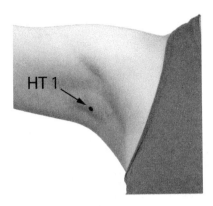

Heart (Ht 1): 극천 : 極泉

Location: With the arm raised, this point can be found in the center of the axilla (arm pit), medial to the axillary artery.

Striking: Straight up into the axilla (arm pit). Straight into the point for best effect, but angles of any direction may still produce a strong effect.

Observed effects of strike: Extreme pain with only a mild strike, numbness and temporary paralysis in the shoulder and arm.

Known effects: Knockout and unconsciousness.

Theoretical effects: This point will affect the shin (spirit) causing a disconnected feeling, impaired mental activity and speech. It is possible to cause death with this point.

Explanation: This channel energy runs down like a mountain spring. The channel energy of the Heart runs down from this point, so this point is the highest spring.

Primary Actions and Functions: Nourishes Heart Um, clears empty heat. Benefits the arm & shoulder. Activates and frees the channel, Loosens the chest.

Korean: Geuk Chun: Summit Spring: 극천

Chinese: Ji Quan: Ji = Highest. Quan = Spring, fountain or the source of a river. 極泉

Japanese: Kyokusen

Special Note: This point can cause Death. This point is also one of the so called **_"delayed death touch"_** points because there is a group of lymph nodes in the arm pit that if ruptured will slowly poison the system causing the person to die slowly. Rupturing of the axillary artery will also cause death but much faster than the lymph node rupture.

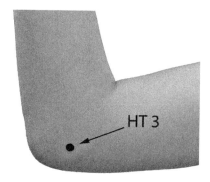

Heart (Ht 3): 소해 : 少海

Location: With the elbow flexed, at the midpoint of the line connecting the medial end of the cubital crease and the medial epicondyle of the humerus.12

Striking: Ninety degrees to the elbow straight in to the point and slightly downward for maximum results. This point is commonly grabbed to apply pressure.

Observed effects of strike: Great pain allowing manipulation of the arm. Numbness in the elbow and lower arm. Confushion from strong pain.

Known effects: Temporary paralysis of the elbow and lower arm.

Theoretical effects: Tendon damage in the elbow. May cause long-term nervous or emotional disorders. This point may cause the immediate heart stoppage and death.

Explanation: The Heart channel of the hand is like a river running into the sea. Shaohai is the ancient name for the "Bohai Sea".

Primary Actions and Functions: Removes obstructions from the channel, calms the mind & clears heat. Clears the Pericardium, Stabilizes the spirit disposition.

Korean: Soh Hae: Lesser Sea: 소해

Chinese: Shao Hai: Shao = The Heart channel of the hand. Hai = Sea or reservoir. 少海

Japanese: Shokai

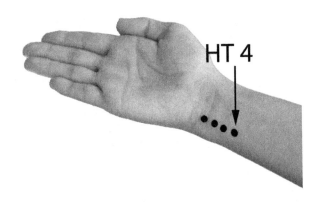

Heart (Ht 4): 영도 : 靈道

Location: When the palm faces upward, the point is 1.5 cun proximal (above) to the distal (lower) wrist crease, on the radial side of the tendon of the flexor carpi ulnaris.

Striking: A strong strike straight into the point. This point is also very effective with proper gripping pressure.

Observed effects of strike: Pain causing numbing of the hand.

Known effects: Damage to the tendon is possible.

Theoretical effects: May cause immediate high blood pressure.

Explanation: This point is the road leading to the normal emotional activities. It is used to treat psychosis.

Primary Actions and Functions: Removes obstructions from the channel. Nourishes the Heart. Calms the spirit and benefits the voice. Relaxes the muscles and sinews.

Korean: Young Doh: Spirit (Mind) Path: 영도

Chinese: Ling Dao: Ling = God, deity, soul, spirit, or heart. Dao = Road, way, channel, or course. 靈道

Japanese: Reido

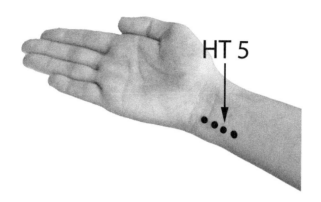

Heart (Ht 5): 통리 : 通里

Location: On the radial side of the tendon of the flexor carpi ulnaris, 1 cun proximal to the distal (lower) wrist crease.

Striking: A strong strike straight into the point. This point is commonly used with grabbing technique.

Observed effects of strike: Pain and hand numbness. Mental confusion.

Known effects: Weakens the arm.

Theoretical effects: It is possible to cause a knockout using this point because of extreme Ki drainage.

Explanation: This point connects with the inside of the Heart channel as well as the Small Intestine channel. It is the connecting point of those two channels. It also goes deep into the abdomen and to the small intestine.

Primary Actions and Functions: Calms the spirit (mind), Regulates the Heart rhythm, Opens into the tongue, Benefits the bladder. Regulates the Heart Ki, Activates the channel and alleviates pain.

Korean: Tong Ri: Penetrating the Interior or Inner Communication: 통리

Chinese: Tong Li: Tong = To unobstruct or clear, lead to or connect. Li = Inside. 通里

Japanese: Tsuri

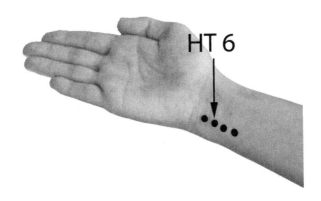

Heart (Ht 6): 음극 : 陰郄

Location: On the radial side of the tendon of the flexor carpi ulnaris, 0.5 cun proximal to the distal wrist crease.

Striking: A strong strike straight into the point. This point is commonly used with grabbing technique.

Observed effects of strike: Pain and numbing in the local wrist area.

Known effects: Hand and local wrist numbness.

Theoretical effects: May weaken the heart and possibly cause mental confusion or even madness.

Explanation: The abbreviated form for the Cleft point of the Heart channel of the hand.

Primary Actions and Functions: Nourishes Heart Yin and Regulates Heart blood, Alleviates night sweating. Calms the Spirit (mind), Clears Heart fire.

Korean: Um Guek: Um Accumulation or Um Cleft (Slit): 음극

Chinese: Yin Xi: Yin = The Heart channel of the hand. Xi = A hole in general or the Cleft point (a storing place for channel energy). 陰郄

Japanese: Ingeki

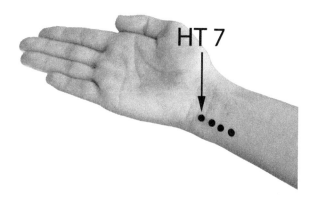

Heart (Ht 7): 신문 : 神門

Location: At the ulnar end of the distal wrist crease, in the depression at the radial side of the flexor carpi ulnaris, at the proximal border of the pisiform bone.

Striking: A strong strike straight into the point. This point is commonly used with grabbing technique.

Observed effects of strike: Pain and bruising in the point area. Can cause hand numbness.

Known effects: May cause electrical sensation traveling into the hand.

Theoretical effects: Possible damage to the wrist joint. Possible emotional instability.

Explanation: Daoist called the eye Shenmen, the gate for the spirit to go in or out.

Primary Actions and Functions: Calms the mind, Nourishes Heart blood and opens orifices. Quiets the Heart and spirit, Clears Heart heat, Tonifies the Heart.

Korean: Shin Moon: Spirit (mind) Gate: 신문

Chinese: Shen Men: Shen = The mind, the state of mind, spirit, the Yang energy of the body. Men = Gate. 神門

Japanese: Shinmon

Special Note: Heart 4, 5, 6, and 7 are very close to each other. Because they are so close to each other it is common for all four points to be hit or grabbed at the same time with one striking or grabbing technique.

THE SMALL INTESTINE CHANNEL

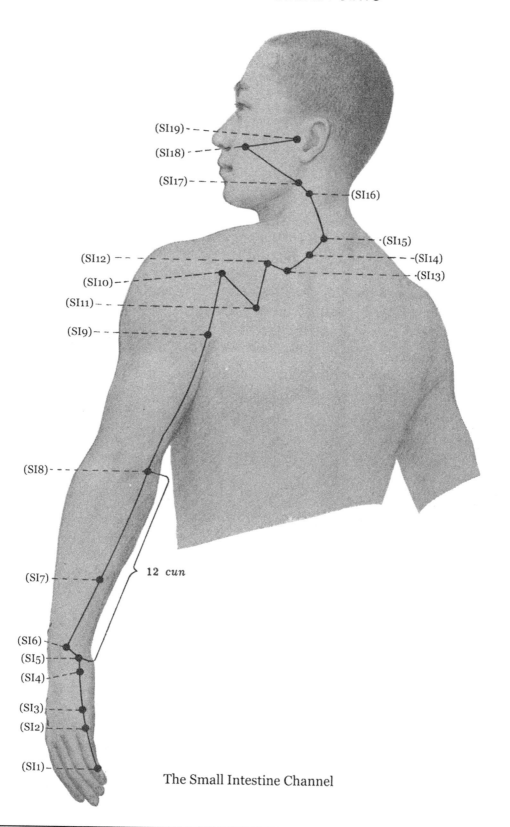

(SI19) - - -
(SI18) - - -
(SI17) - - -
(SI16)
(SI15)
(SI14)
(SI13)
(SI12) - - -
(SI10) - - -
(SI11) - - -
(SI9) - - -
(SI8) - - -
12 *cun*
(SI7) - - -
(SI6) -
(SI5) -
(SI4) -
(SI3) - -
(SI2) - -
(SI1) -

The Small Intestine Channel

Superficial pathway and measurement on the body

For Small Intestine channel flow and functions see page 186.

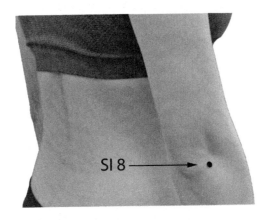

Small Intestine (SI 8): 소해 : 小海

Location: When the elbow is flexed, the point is located in the depression between the olecranon of the ulna and the medial epicondyle of the humerus.

Striking: Straight in to the point inside the elbow. This point is commonly used for grabbing and manipulating.

Observed effects of strike: Great pain with strong pressure or striking. Strong pressure may bring the person to the ground causing the legs to collapse. Numbness and temporary paralysis may occur with grabbing or striking technique.

Known effects: Ki drainage of the arm causing weakness. May cause a headache.

Theoretical effects: This point may cause knockout due to the shock. It is said that this point can also cause death.

Explanation: The sea formed by the energy of the Small Intestine channel.

Primary Actions and Functions: Clears heat and dissipates swelling, Calms the spirit. Activates the channel and alleviates pain, Dispels wind Ki.

Korean: Soh Hae: Small Sea (Small Intestine Sea): 소해

Chinese: Xiao Hai: Xiao = The Small Intestine channel of the hand. Hai = The sea or ocean. 小海

Japanese: Shokai

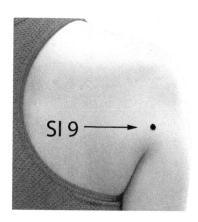

Small Intestine (SI 9): 견정 : 肩貞

Location: Posterior and inferior to the shoulder joint. When the arm is adducted, the point is 1 cun above the posterior end of the axillary fold.

Location Note: With the arm hanging freely at the side, this point is found 1 cun directly above the posterior axillary crease (rear armpit crease), just below the posterior border of the deltoid.

Striking: Straight in to the point or slightly upwards. Also, finger pressure is used on this point to manipulate shoulder direction.

Observed effects of strike: Pain and loss of shoulder movement.

Known effects: Dislocated shoulder

Theoretical effects: This point may cause nausea and fainting.

Explanation: This point is in the position where the vital energy of the shoulder is stationed to prevent invasion of foreign evils.

Primary Actions and Functions: Expels wind and benefits the shoulder, activates the channel and alleviates pain. Dissipates, binds and relieves pain.

Korean: Gyun Jung: True Shoulder or Upright Shoulder: 견정

Chinese: Jian Zhen: Jian = Shoulder. Zhen = Vital energy. 肩貞

Japanese: Kentei

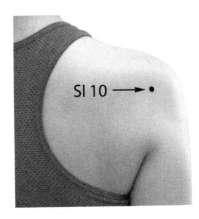

Small Intestine (SI 10): 뇌유 : 臑俞

Location: On the posterior aspect of the shoulder, in the depression inferior to the scapular spine, directly superior to the posterior axillary crease when the arm hangs in the adducted position.

Location Note: Slide a finger directly upwards from Gyun Jung (Si 9), until it falls into the depression just below the scapular spine.

Striking: Straight into the point or slightly upward. Finger pressure can be used on this point to manipulate the shoulder.

Observed effects of strike: Pain and numbness of the shoulder.

Known effects: Dislocation of shoulder joint, scapula damage, local tendon and ligament damage.

Theoretical effects: Knockout is also possible with this point.

Explanation: The pivot of the shoulder muscles. This part is irrigated by the channel energy of the upper arm.

Primary Actions and Functions: Benefits the shoulder, activates the channel and alleviates pain. Quickens the blood and frees the connecting vessels, soothes the sinews and dissipates binding.

Korean: Noe Yoo: Humerus Transporting Point or Upper Arm Yoo (Scapula's Hollow): 뇌유

Chinese: Nao Shu: Nao = Muscles below the shoulder. Shu = Pivot or convey. 臑俞

Japanese: Juyu

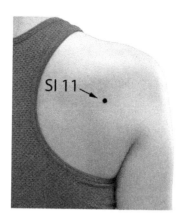

Small Intestine (SI 11): 천종 : 天宗

Location: On the scapula, in a tender depression one third of the distance from the midpoint of the inferior border of the scapular spine to the inferior angle of the scapula. In the infrascuplar fossa (hole in the scapula).

Location Note: This point may be quite difficult to palpate (feel). Another way to locate this point is to draw an equilateral triangle with Gyun Jung (Si 9) and Noe Yoo (Si 10) after first ensuring that the persons shoulder is relaxed. Try to feel the small hole or indentation in the scupla.

Striking: Straight in to the point gives the best effect.

Observed effects of strike: Pain in the scapula and shoulder area. Electrical shock running down the outside of the arm all the way through the little finger. Inability to move the shoulder and arm.

Known effects: Temporary paralysis of the shoulder, arm and hand.

Theoretical effects: This point can cause great damage both physical and energetic throughout the shoulder, back and arm. Paralysis may last a long time.

Explanation: This point is the name of a constellation. It is also a general form referring to the celestial phenomena. This point is surrounded and worshiped by a number of points that are arranged in the form of a constellation.

Primary Actions and Functions: Activates the channel and alleviates pain. Diffuses Ki stagnation in the chest and lateral costal region.

Korean: Chun Jong: Heavenly Gathering or Heaven's Ancestor: 천종

Chinese: Tian Zong: Tian = Heaven, sky or the upper part of the human body. 天宗
Zong = Worship.

Japanese: Tenso

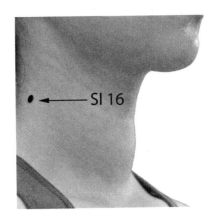

Small Intestine (SI 16): 천창 : 天窓

Location: On the posterior border of the sternocleidomastoid muscle, level with the laryngeal (Adams-apple) prominence.

Striking: Straight in to the point from the side of the neck is the most effective. Also this point can be hit at any angel and produce an effective result.

Observed effects of strike: Brain confusion, blurry vision. Knockout and unconsciousness.

Known effects: Temporary loss of vision.

Theoretical effects: Hit with enough power this point can produce coma and death.

Explanation: This point is compared to the window of the upper part of the human body because this point can be used to treat diseases of the orifices in the face and the head (eye, mouth, nose, and ear).

Primary Actions and Functions: Benefits the ears, throat, and voice. Regulates Ki, activates the channel and alleviates pain and clears heat. Calms the spirit and nourishes the Heart.

Korean: Chun Chang: Heavenly (celestial) Window: 천창

Chinese: Tian Chuang: Tian = Heaven, sky, the upper part of the human body. Chuang = Window for ventilation. 天窓

Japanese: Tenso

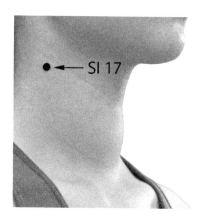

Small Intestine (SI 17): 천용 : 天容

Location: Posterior to the angle of the mandible (jaw), in the depression at the anterior border of the sternocleidomastoid muscle.

Striking: Strike slightly upward and straight in to the point for maximum effect. This point will also be very effective if hit from any angle.

Observed effects of strike: Disorientation, knockout.

Known effects: Since it's close to the carotid artery, this point can cause blood flow problems to the brain.

Theoretical effects: This point can also cause death if hit with enough power.

Explanation: This point is on the neck. The neck supports the head and keeps one's personal appearance. The neck of the ancient warrior was protected with a hood behind the neck or helmet.

Primary Actions and Functions: Descends rebellious Ki, Benefits the ears and removes obstructions from the channel. Benefits the neck and throat and disperses swelling. Soothes the sinews.

Korean: Chun Yong: Heavenly Appearance or Heaven's Contents: 천용

Chinese: Tian Rong: Tian = Heaven, sky or the upper part of the human body.

Rong = Appearance, or a means for protecting the body. 天容

Japanese: Tenyo

THE URINARY BLADDER CHANNEL

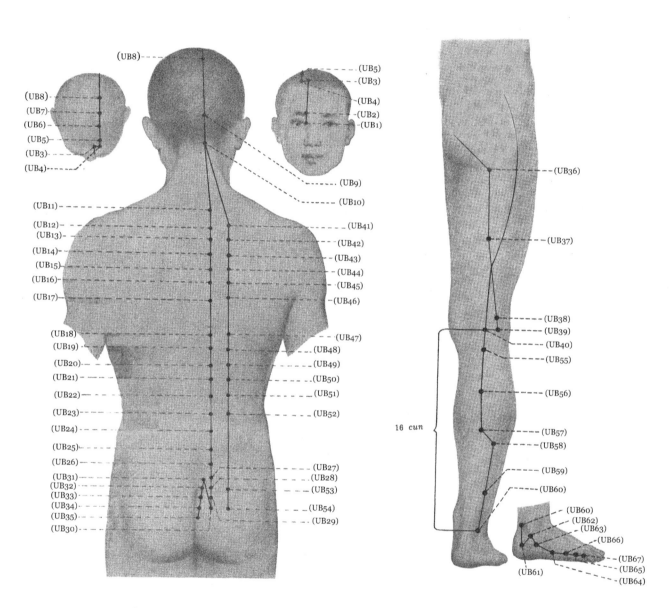

The Urinary Bladder Channel

The Urinary Bladder Channel

Superficial pathway and measurement on the body

For Urinary Bladder channel flow and functions see page 187.

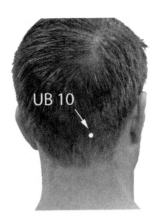

Urinary Bladder (UB 10): 천주 : 天柱

Location: 1.3 cun lateral to the midpoint of the posterior (back) hairline and in the depression on the lateral aspect of the trapezius muscle. Located 1.3 cun lateral to Governing 15 which is also on the midline.

Striking: Strike straight in to the point for best results but any angle will have strong effect. This point can also be used with grabbing techniques for effective results.

Observed effects of strike: Great pain. A very light strike causes headache and vision problems. It will also cause disorientation and temporary loss of vision.

Known effects: A medium to hard strike will cause knockout and unconsciousness.

Theoretical effects: This point will cause coma or death with a very hard strike.

Explanation: This point is on the neck that is the pillar of the head. Pillar of the heaven is also the name for a mountain and for a star.

Primary Actions and Functions: Clears the brain, Removes obstructions from the channel, brightens the eyes and invigorates the lower back. Regulates Ki and pacifies wind. Relieves pain and Calms the spirit.

Korean: Chun Joo: Celestial (heavens) Pillar: 천주

Chinese: Tian Zhu: Tian = Sky, heaven or head. Zhu = Pillar. 天柱

Japanese: Tenchu

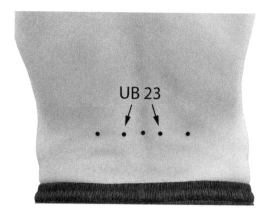

Urinary Bladder (UB 23): 신유 : 腎俞

Location: At the level of the lower border of the spinous process of the second lumbar vertebra. 1.5 cun lateral to Governing 4 (Myung Moon), which is at the midline of the spine.

Special Note about Location: This point is located on the waist line level with the umbilical (navel).

Striking: Strike straight into the point. Also an upward or downward strike produces strong results.

Observed effects of strike: Extreme pain that can cause the legs to collapse.

Known effects: A strong enough strike may cause blood in the urine.

Theoretical effects: A very strong strike may cause kidney failure and possible death.

Explanation: This point leads to the Kidney. The kidney stores up the essence of the vital organs of the human body and it is responsible for water which is used to irrigate the whole body. This point has the function of drawing water and storing up the essence.

Primary Actions and Functions: Tonifies Kidneys and nourishes the Kidney essence, strengthens the lower back, nourishes blood, benefits bone and marrow. It strengthens the Kidney function of reception of Ki. Strengthens the Lumbar and spine. Brightens the eyes and sharpens the hearing.

Korean: Shin Yoo: Kidney's Hollow (Yoo): 신유

Chinese: Shen Shu: Shen = Kidney. Shu = Pivot or convey. 腎俞

Japanese: Jinyu

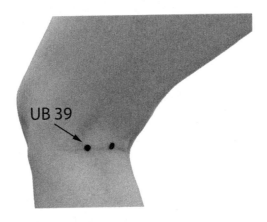

Urinary Bladder (UB 39): 위양 : 委陽

Location: At the back of the knee, on the popliteal crease and towards its lateral end, in the depression medial to the tendon of the medial biceps femoris.

Striking: Straight in to the point with a hand strike or kick. This point is also used in grabbing technique.

Observed effects of strike: Great leg pain, bruising, numbness, and swelling, causing inability to move the knee and walk. Pain can get worse without treatment.

Known effects: Tendon, muscle, and ligament damage to the knee.

Theoretical effects: Immediate, uncontrolled urination. May cause damage to the bladder.

Explanation: This point is lateral to the (Weizhong) point Urinary Bladder 40, which is in the center of the hollow of the knee.

Primary Actions and Functions: Opens the water passages in the Lower Burner and benefits the bladder. Harmonizes the Triple Burner and regulates urination. Activates the channel and alleviates pain.

Korean: Wee Yang: Outside of the Crook or Supporting Yang or Bent Yang or Spirits Hall: 위양

Chinese: Wei Yang: Wei = Flex or lie down. Yang = The lateral side. 委陽

Japanese: Iyo

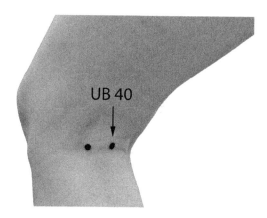

Urinary Bladder (UB 40): 위중 : 委中

Location: In the middle of the back of the knee. In the middle of the Popliteal fossa on the transverse crease, between the tendons of muscle biceps femoris and muscle semitendinosus.

Striking: Strike this point straight in with a hand strike or kick. This point is also used in grabbing techniques.

Observed effects of strike: Great pain in local area, spasms, numbness, and inability to use the knee and walk. Pain can get worse without treatment.

Known effects: Damage of muscles, ligaments, and tendons in the knee area. Possible damage to the artery located behind the point if the strike is hard enough.

Theoretical effects: This point can shock the body to the point of knockout.

Explanation: In order to get to this point, the subject should lie down on his face with his knee flexed. The point is in the center of the hollow of the back of the knee.

Primary Actions and Functions: Cools the blood, relaxes the sinews, eliminates stasis of blood, and clears summer heat. Benefits the lumbar region and knees

Korean: Wee Joong: Middle of the crook, Supporting middle or Bent middle: 위중

Chinese: Wei Zhong: Wei = Flex or to lie down. Zhong = Middle or center. 委中

Japanese: Ichu

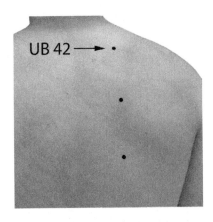

Urinary Bladder (UB 42): 백호 : 魄戶

Location: 3 Cun lateral to the midline of the spine, at the level of the lower border of the spinous process of the second thoracic vertebra, on the medial border of the scapula.

Striking: Strike straight in to the point with a hand strike or kick.

Observed effects of strike: Knocks the wind out of the individual.

Known effects: May damage the structure of the upper body.

Theoretical effects: May drain enough energy from the body to cause it to collapse. A sharp strike may send a shock wave through the heart possibly causing it to flutter or even to stop.

Explanation: This point is the gate defending the vigor of the lung. This point is lateral to the Urinary Bladder 13 (Feishu) and dependent on Urinary Bladder 13 (Feishu). This point also defends the vigor of the lung.

Primary Actions and Functions: Regulates Ki, Stimulates the descending of Lung Ki. Calms dyspnea and suppresses cough.

Korean: Baek Ho: Soul's Door or Door of the Corporeal Soul: 백호

Chinese: Po Hu: Po = The Yin (Um) God accompanying the vigor that belongs to the lung. Hu = Gate, door or household. 魄戶

Japanese: Hakko

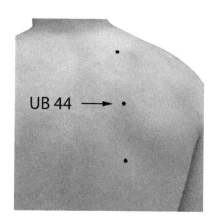

Urinary Bladder (UB 44): 신당 : 神堂

Location: 3 cun lateral to the midline of the spine at the level of the lower border of the spinous process of the fifth thoracic vertebra, on the spinal border of the scapula.

Striking: Strike straight in to this point with a hand strike or a kick.

Observed effects of strike: Knocks the wind out of the individual.

Known effects: A powerful enough strike may shock the Lung enough to cause the person to collapse or knock them out.

Theoretical effects: May have a strong effect on a person's will power, causing them great difficulty in matters of will power and a feeling of being disconnected spiritually.

Explanation: This point is compared to the hall where the monarch of the Heart holds court. The Heart keeps vital Yang energy, it is the supreme, and it is the monarch.

Primary Actions and Functions: Unbinds the chest and regulates the Ki. Activates the channel and alleviates pain. Calms the Mind

Korean: Shin Dahng: Wills Residence, Spirit's Hall or Mind Hall: 신당

Chinese: Shen Tang: Shen = The vital energy symbolizing the monarch. Tang = Hall or palace. 神堂

Japanese: Shindo

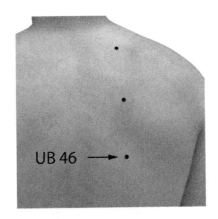

Urinary Bladder (UB 46): 격관 : 膈關

Location: 3 Cun lateral to the midline of the spine, level with the lower border of the spinous process of the seventh thoracic vertebra, approximately at the level of the lower border of the scapula.

Striking: Straight in to the point or slightly upward towards the scapula using a hand strike or kick.

Observed effects of strike: Pain, wind knocked out of the individual.

Known effects: Damage to the structure of the upper body with a hard strike.

Theoretical effects: May cause instant spasm that drops the person to the ground.

Explanation: This point is the passage of the diaphragm, it can open the road block. This point is lateral to Urinary Bladder 17 (Geshu). In fact, it is dependent on Urinary Bladder 17. The functions of the two points are closely related.

Primary Actions and Functions: Regulates the diaphragm, benefits the middle burner, activates the channel and alleviates pain. Fortifies the spleen and harmonizes the stomach.

Korean: Kyuk Gwan: Vital's Door, Diaphragm Gate or Diaphragm's Pass: 격관

Chinese: Ge Guan: Ge = The Diaphragm. Guan = Gate, passage or block. 膈關

Japanese: Kakukan

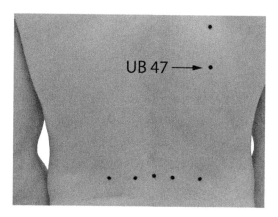

Urinary Bladder (UB 47): 혼문 : 魂門

Location: 3 Cun lateral to the midline of the spine at the lower border of the spinous process of the ninth thoracic vertebra.

Striking: Straight in to the point with a hand strike or kick.

Observed effects of strike: Pain and collapse of the body.

Known effects: May have damaging effects on the lung.

Theoretical effects: It is said that this point may cause behavioral problems because of its effect on the spirit or soul of the individual. May also affect the individual's will power.

Explanation: This point is the gate through which the Yang energy of the liver gets in or out. It is also the gate safeguarding the liver's Yang energy for the soul, spirit or essence of the Yang energy.

Primary Actions and Functions: Regulates Liver Ki and roots the ethereal soul. Relaxes the sinews and harmonizes the middle burner. Frees and regulates bowel Ki.

Korean: Hohn Moon: Will's Door, Gate or Door of the Ethereal Soul, 혼문

Chinese: Hun Men: Hun = Soul, spirit or the essence of the vital Yang energy of the human body. Men = Gate or safeguard. 魂門

Japanese: Konmon

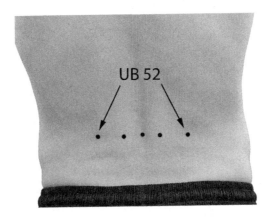

Urinary Bladder (UB 52): 지실 : 志室

Location: 3 cun lateral to the midline, level with the lower border of the spinous process of the second lumbar vertebra and level with UB 23 (Shin Yoo).

Striking: Strike straight in with a hand strike or kick.

Observed effects of strike: Extreme pain, inability to stand up.

Known effects: Injury to the back muscles.

Theoretical effects: Damages the will power of the individual to do anything.

Explanation: The "Will" can be in full play only when the Kidney is filled up with vital energy.

Primary Actions and Functions: Tonifies the Kidneys, strengthens the back, and reinforces the will power. Supplements the Kidneys and boosts essence and regulates urination.

Korean: Jee Shil: Will Power Chamber, Residence of the "Will", or Floating Ki: 지실

Chinese: Zhi Shi: Zhi = The will or the vital energy of the Kidney. Shi = Room or fill up. 志室

Japanese: Shishitsu

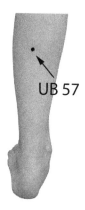

Urinary Bladder (UB 57): 승산 : 承山

Location: On the posterior (back) of the leg, in a pointed depression formed below the gastrocnemius muscle belly when the leg is stretched or the heel is lifted.

Striking: Straight in to the point with a hand strike or kick.

Observed effects of strike: Extreme pain and swelling in the lower leg. Inability to stand or put weight on the leg. Can paralyze the lower leg.

Known effects: If the strike is severe enough, the individual may need medical treatment to recover from damage.

Theoretical effects: May cause the brain to become temporarily confused so it cannot figure out where the pain is coming from.

Explanation: This point is between the "sural" (calf of the leg) muscles that bear the tall and heavy mountain of the body.

Primary Actions and Functions: Relaxes the sinews, invigorates blood, removes obstructions and clears heat from the channel. Activates the channel and alleviates pain, Benefits the calf and heel and treats hemorrhoids.

Korean: Seung Sahn: Support the Mountain: 승산

Chinese: Cheng Shan: Cheng = Receive. Shan = Mountain, referring to the body that is tall and heavy. 承山

Japanese: Shozan

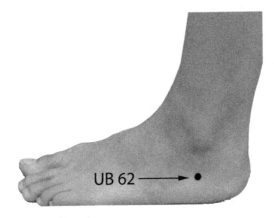

Urinary Bladder (UB 62): 신맥 : 申脈

Location: In the depression directly below the external malleolus. On the lateral side of the foot, approximately 0.5 cun inferior (below) to the inferior border of the lateral malleolus, in a depression posterior to the peroneal tendons.

Striking: Straight in to the point with a kick or hand strike.

Observed effects of strike: Extreme pain, swelling, and inability to stand on that foot. Pain can get worse without treatment.

Known effects: A strong enough strike can cause tendon and nerve damage.

Theoretical effects: May cause great anger and mental disorders due to the rapid rise of Yang Ki to the head.

Explanation: This point can be used to treat the stiffness or feebleness of the limbs, so they can flex and stretch freely and forcefully. This point belongs to the Urinary Bladder channel. The hour of "Shen" is the peak period of the vital energy of the bladder.

Primary Actions and Functions: Calms the spirit, Benefits the head and eyes and opens and regulates the Yang Motility vessel (meridian). Activates the channel and alleviates pain. Stabilizes the spirit disposition and soothes the sinews and vessels.

Korean: Shin Maek: Extending Vessel (Ninth Channel): 신맥

Chinese: Shen Mai: Shen = To extend, stretch, groan or the period of the day from 3pm to 5pm. Mai = Tendons and muscles. 申脈

Japanese: Shinmyaku

THE KIDNEY CHANNEL

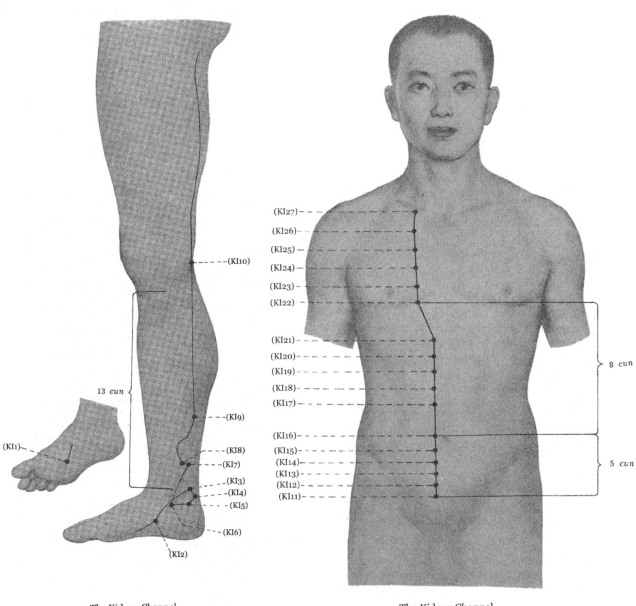

The Kidney Channel

The Kidney Channel

Superficial pathway and measurement on the body

For Kidney channel flow and functions see page 188.

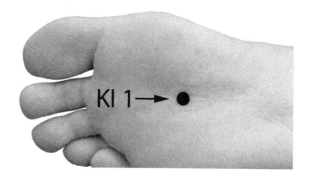

Kidney (Ki 1): 용천 : 涌泉

Location: On the sole of the foot in the depression when the foot is in plantar flexion, approximately at the junction of the anterior third and posterior two thirds of the line connecting the base of the 2nd and 3rd toes and the heel.

Striking: This point is very difficult to get to, but if you can get to it a strong hand strike or kick will be effective.

Observed effects of strike: Pain in the foot sometimes strong enough to prevent the individual from walking. Revival of a passed-out individual by striking the point.

Known effects: A strong enough strike can cause damage to the foot bones.

Theoretical effects: It is possible to deliver a knockout blow striking this point. In old Korea, one punishment was hanging a person upside down with their bare feet exposed and beating the bottom of the feet with a wooden paddle. It is said that people would sometimes die from this punishment of hitting the bottom of the feet. It was said that the damage to Kidney 1 was the reason for their death.

Special Note for Application: In martial art this point is used when there is too much Yang Ki rushing to the head causing extreme dizziness or passing out. For resuscitation when someone passes out due to overheating this point is pressed sharply or hit strongly several times causing the Ki to come down and the individual to recover. This point may also resuscitate someone that has been knocked out by a strike. This point may also be used to restart the heart if CPR doesn't work.

Explanation: This point is on the sole of the foot. The channel energy goes up like water gushing up in a spring or fountain.

Primary Actions and Functions: Tonifies the Um, calms the mind, restores consciousness and clears the brain. It also subdues wind and clears heat. Descends excess heat from the head, stabilizes the spirit disposition and brings down Um fire.

Korean: Yong Chun: Gushing Spring or Bubbling Spring: 용천

Chinese: Yong Quan: Yong = To gush out or well up. Quan = Spring or fountain. 涌泉

Japanese: Yusen

Special Note: This point is also important in meditation because it receives the earth's Ki from the ground through the point Kidney 1. In "Ki Gong" practice ("chi gong" in chinese), directing the mind to Kidney 1 (Yong Chun) or inhaling and exhaling through this point, roots and descends the Ki in the "Dahn Jun" (lower abdomen or Ki Box) and helps the body absorb the Um (Yin) energy of the earth.

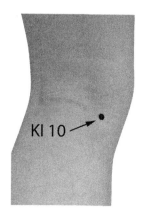

Kidney (Ki 10): 음곡 : 陰谷

Location: When the knee is flexed, the point is behind the knee on the medial side of the popliteal fossa, between the tendons of muscle semitendinosus and semimembranosus, at the level with Urinary Bladder 40 (Wee Joong).

Striking: Straight in to the back of the knee. This point is also used for grabbing technique.

Observed effects of strike: Pain and swelling in back of the knee limiting the movement of the knee. Temporary paralysis in knee

Known effects: Damage to the tendon and ligaments in the back of the knee.

Theoretical effects: This point can cause a knockout. It may cause kidney failure either immediately or by slow degeneration of the kidneys. Because of this type of damage this point may cause death.

Explanation: This point is in the valley-like depression at the medial side of the knee. It is used to treat diseases caused by wind evils in the lower limbs.

Primary Actions and Functions: Benefits the Kidney and tonifies Kidney Um. Expels dampness from the Lower Burner. Activates the channel and alleviates pain. Dispels damp and frees urine.

Korean: Um Gohk: Um Valley: 음곡

Chinese: Yin Gu: Yin = Inner side or medial side. Gu = Valley or name of a wind. 陰谷

Japanese: Inkoku

THE PERICARDIUM CHANNEL

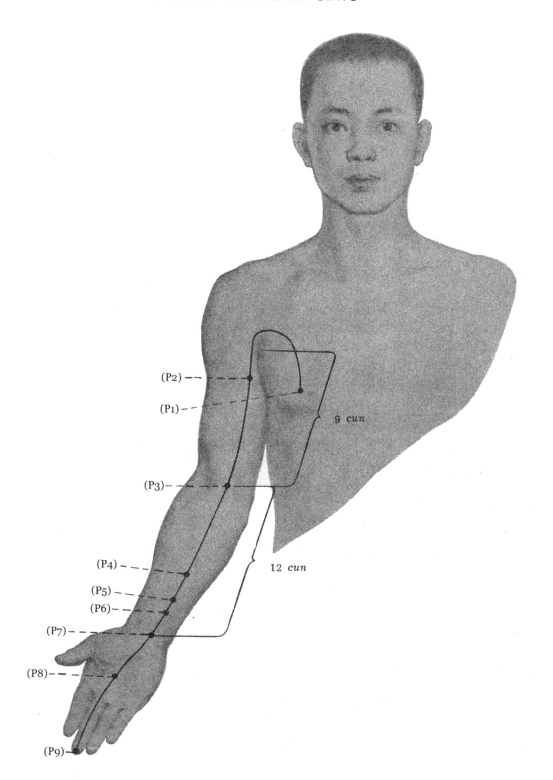

The Pericardium Channel

Superficial pathway and measurement on the body

For Pericardium channel flow and functions see page 189.

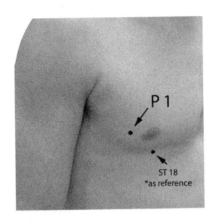

Pericardium (P 1): 천지 : 天池

Location: One cun lateral and slightly superior to the nipple, in the 4th intercostal space.

Striking: Straight in to the point or slightly angled towards the middle of the chest with a hand strike or a kick.

Observed effects of strike: Pain and knock down or knock out from the strike.

Known effects: Continuing chest pain after the strike.

Theoretical effects: This point may affect the emotions. This point may also cause heart problems and even heart attack causing death.

Explanation: The milk storing breast is compared to Heavens Pool. The point is on the breast near the nipple. "Tianchi" is also the name for a great sea, a mountain and a star.

Primary Actions and Functions: Regulates Ki and dissipates nodules. Benefits the breasts, unbinds the chest, transforms phlegm and descends rebellion. Opens the chest and rectifies Ki. Suppresses cough and calms dyspnea. Diffused the Lung and clears heat.

Korean: Chun Ji: Heaven's Pool or Pond: 천지

Chinese: Tian Chi: Tian = The upper part of the human body or sky or heaven. Chi = Pool. 天池

Japanese: Tenchi

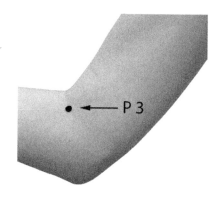

Pericardium (P 3): 곡택 : 曲澤

Location: On the transverse cubital crease, at the ulnar side of the tendon of the muscle biceps brachii.

Striking: This point is most often used in grabbing techniques. For striking, hit straight in to the point with a hand strike.

Observed effects of strike: Local pain and elbow numbness with a strong grab. Inability to move the elbow with a direct strike.

Known effects: A strong strike creates the inability to use that arm and may damage the tendons and ligaments.

Theoretical effects: May negatively affect the lung as well at the heart with a very strong strike.

Explanation: This point is located in the shallow depression of the elbow.

Primary Actions and Functions: Activates the channel and alleviates pain. Opens the orifices, stops convulsions, moves blood and dispels stasis. Calms the mind and pacifies the Stomach. Clears heat from the Ki, nutritive and blood levels. Harmonizes the Stomach and intestines and stops vomiting.

Korean: Gohk Taek: Marsh at the Crook: 곡택

Chinese: Qu Ze: Qu = Crooked or flex. Ze = Depression or indentation. 曲澤

Japanese: Kyokutaku

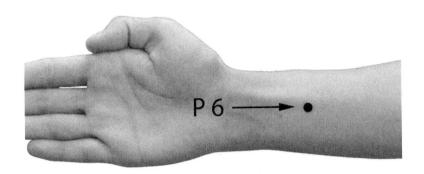

Pericardium (P 6): 내관 : 內關

Location: two cun above the transverse crease of the wrist, between the tendons of muscle palmaris longus and muscle flexor carpi radialis.

Striking: Straight in to the point usually with a hand strike. This point is also a common point for grabbing techniques.

Observed effects of strike: Pain and inability to use the hand if hit hard enough. Can take the power out of a persons grip.

Known effects: This point may cause mental confusion especially if gripped hard enough.

Theoretical effects: May cause strong nausea and the individual to turn green and vomit.

Explanation: This point is at an important place on the inner side of the forearm. It has the function of curing diseases of the diaphragm and block actions such as vomiting and hiccupping. This point corresponds to Triple Bruner 5 (waiguan). The two points are interrelated. It dwells in both the Lung and Heart channel. It is also an important place connecting the hand Pericardium and Triple Burner channel.

Primary Actions and Functions: Unbinds the chest and regulates Ki. Regulates the Heart and clams the spirit. Harmonizes the Stomach and alleviates nausea and vomiting. Clears heat and opens the Um (yin) linking vessel. Loosens the chest and rectifies Ki. Harmonizes the stomach and relieves pain.

Korean: Nae Gwan: Internal gate or Inner Pass: 내관

Chinese: Nei Guan: Nei = In the diaphragm, the inner side of the forearm or inner. Guan = Block or passage. 內關

Japanese: Naikan

Special Note: This point can help calm or cure nausea and vomiting when messaged or pressed firmly. It's also a point to help calm headache pain.

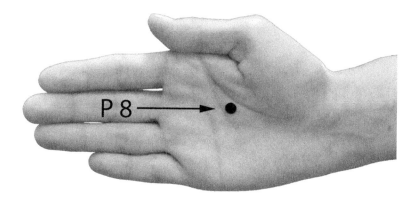

Pericardium (P 8): 노궁 : 勞宮

Location: Between the second and third metacarpal bones, proximal to the metacarpo-phalangeal joint, in a depression at the radial side of the third metacarpal bone. This point may be located at the place where the tip of the middle finger lands when a fist is made. Some classical sources locate this point on the ulnar side of the third metacarpal bone, where the tip of the ring finger lands when a fist is made.

Striking: Straight in to the point.

Observed effects of strike: Pain and bruising.

Known effects: Damage to the hand.

Theoretical effects: It is possible for this point to cause heart problems.

Explanation: This point is used to treat diseases that affect the manipulative labor of the hand. It is in the center of the palm. That location is a very important place.

Primary Actions and Functions: Clears heat from the Pericardium and revives consciousness. Clears heat from the Heart and clams the spirit. Harmonizes the Stomach and clears heat from the middle burner.

Korean: No Goong: Labor Palace or Palace of Toil: 노궁

Chinese: Lao Gong: Lao = To work, labor or toil. Gong = Palace. 勞宮

Japanese: Rokyu

Special Note: This point is known for where the Ki emanates from. This Ki is used for both healing and for martial art purposes. This point is also one of the points that receives Ki from the universe when sitting in the meditation posture with the palms up.

THE TRIPLE BURNER CHANNEL

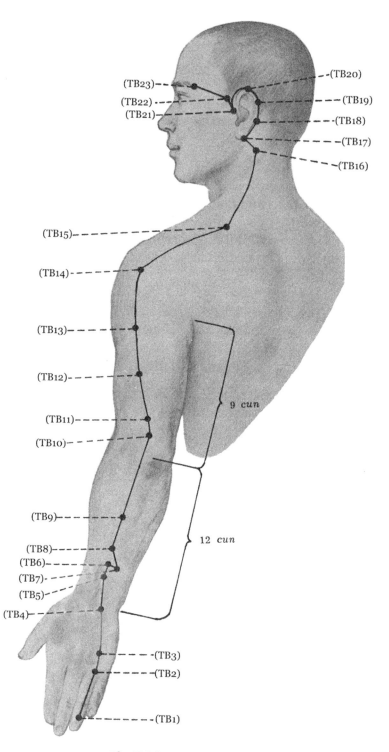

The Triple Burner Channel

Superficial pathway and measurement on the body

For Triple Burner channel flow and functions see page 189.

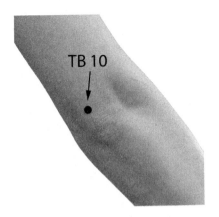

Triple Burner (TB 10): 천정 : 天井

Location: When the elbow is flexed, the point is in the depression about 1 cun superior to the olecranon (tip of elbow).

Striking: Straight in to the point. This point is also used as a point to press into against a straight elbow to take down the opponent.

Observed effects of strike: Pain and swelling from excessive pressure. Damage to the elbow.

Known effects: Broken elbow.

Theoretical effects: May take power away from the legs causing extreme leg weakness and may cause continuous headaches.

Explanation: The water of the heaven well, the name of a constellation or a kind of topography. The channel energy of the upper limb is clean and pure like well water. This point is above the elbow with a tall surrounding and a hollow center, looking like a well, i.e. a well of heaven.

Primary Actions and Functions: Relaxes tendons, Regulates Nutritive and Defensive Qi. Activates the channel and alleviates pain. Calms the spirit. Transforms phlegm damp in the channels and connecting vessels. Clears fire Ki in the Triple burner.

Korean: Chun Jung: Heavenly or Celestial Well: 천정

Chinese: Tian Jing: Tian = Upper limbs, sky or heaven. Jing = Well. 天井

Japanese: Tensei

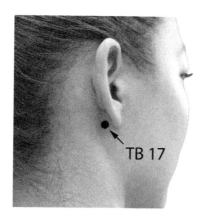

Triple Bruner (TB 17): 예풍 : 翳風

Location: Behind the earlobe in the depression between the mastoid process and the lower jaw.

Striking: Straight in to the point or angle the strike towards the front. This point is also used for grabbing technique especially to cause great pain and exercise control.

Observed effects of strike. Great pain, possible headache, and blurred vision even with a light strike and a little stronger strike will cause a knockout.

Known effects: Ear and hearing damage from a medium to strong strike.

Theoretical effects: A very strong strike especially angled towards the front may cause death.

Explanation: This point is near the upper rim of the collar. The place of sheltering from the wind evil.

Primary Actions and Functions: Benefits the ears, eliminates wind, Clears heat and Activates the channel and alleviates pain. Frees portals and sharpens the hearing. Corrects what is not straight.

Korean: Yea Poong: Sheltering Wind or Wind Screen: 예풍

Chinese: Yi Feng: Yi = Shelter or chest armor. Feng = Wind or wind evil. 翳風

Japanese: Eifu

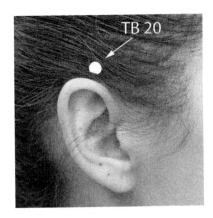

Triple Burner (TB 20): 각손 : 角孫

Location: On the side of the head, directly level with the apex of the ear when the ear is folded forwards. Directly above the ear apex, within the hair line.

Striking: Straight in to the point.

Observed effects of strike: Pain, dizziness, and knockout.

Known effects: May cause nausea with a substantial but less-than-knockout strike.

Theoretical effects: A strong enough strike may cause death.

Explanation: This point is on the corner of the head where a young shoot of horn or antler were to grow out. This arrangement of the point looks like that of the "Jiao" constellation. It also symbolizes the initiation of "Shaoyang" (lesser yang) energy, which is young and feeble and not prosperous yet.

Primary Actions and Functions: Benefits the ears. Benefits the teeth, gums and lips. Clears the head and brightens the eyes. Alleviates pain and clears heat.

Korean: Gahk Sohn: Angle of Regeneration or Minute Angle (Vertex): 각손

Chinese: Jiao Sun: Jiao = Corner or two rear corners above the ears on top of the head where a child's hair was twisted in a knot in ancient times. This point is also the name of a constellation or horn or antler. Sun = Young and feeble or young shoot of something (such as bamboo or deer antler). 角孫

Japanese: Kakuson

Special Note: "Gahk" may mean where a child's hair was twisted in a knot in ancient times. It's also the name of a constellation or horn or antler. "Sohn" can mean young and feeble or the young shoot of something (such as bamboo). Gahk Sohn is on the corner of the head where a young shoot of horn or antler were to grow out. It also symbolizes the initiation of Lesser Yang energy, which is young and feeble or not prosperous yet.

THE GALL BLADDER CHANNEL

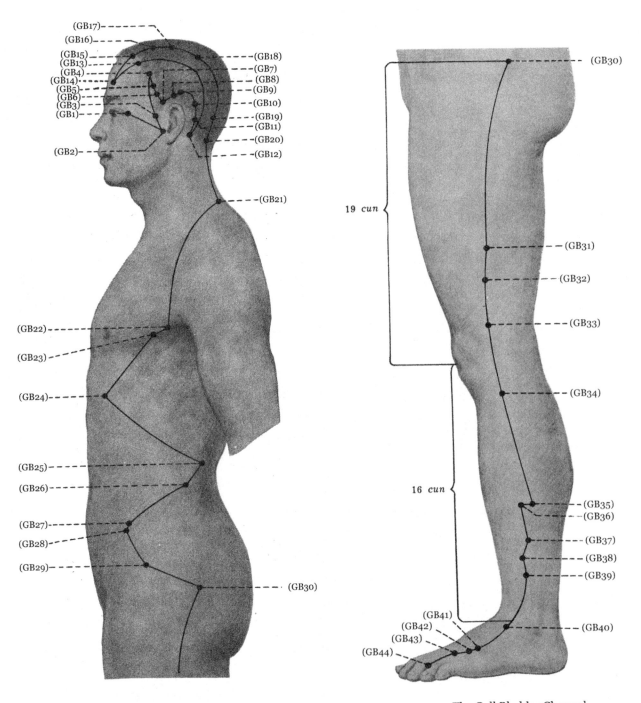

The Gall Bladder Channel

The Gall Bladder Channel

Superficial pathway and measurement on the body

For Gall Bladder channel flow and functions see page 190.

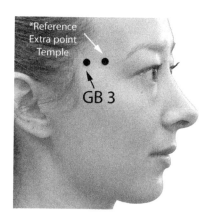

Gall Bladder (GB 3): 객주인 : 上關

Location: Anterior (front) to the ear, in a hollow above the upper border of the zygomatic arch, directly superior (above) to point Stomach 7. First locate Stomach 7 at the lower border of the zygomatic arch, in the depression anterior to the condyloid process of the mandible. Then run the palpating finger superiorly over the zygomatic arch into the hollow for Gall Bladder 3.

Special Note about the Name: In some books I have seen Gall Bladder 3 located at the Temple. However, the Temple is actually a point called "Dae Yang or Big Yang" which is an extra point not a regular point. Gall Bladder 3 is approximately half way between the Temple (Dae Yang) and the front of the ear in a very small hollow just above the zygomatic arch.

Striking: Strike straight in to the point with a hand strike or kick. Pressing into the point can also cause great pain.

Observed effects of strike. Pressing may cause headache and a light strike will cause great pain. A medium strike may cause loss of awareness, muddled thinking, or a complete knockout.

Known effects: A knockout with a long and difficult recovery.

Theoretical effects: This point may cause permanent damage or even death.

Explanation: This point is in front of the ear above the joint of the jaw and the zygomatic arch. It is opposite to Stomach 7.

Primary Actions and Functions: Eliminates wind and benefits to ears. It also activates the channel and alleviates pain. Frees the channels, quickens the connecting and boost hearing.

Korean: Gaek Joo In: Upper Hinge or Above the Joint: 객주인

Alternate Korean Name: Sahng Gwan: Upper Hinge

Chinese: Shang Guan: Shang = Upper. Guan = Joint. 上關

Japanese: Jyokan

Special Note: This is one of the points that a baseball helmet protects to help keep the batting person safe from a baseball strike to the head. This point as well as the temple point can kill if hit with enough force with an object.

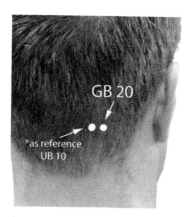

Gall Bladder (GB 20): 풍지 : 風池

Location: Below the occiput, in the hollow between the origins of the sternomastoid and trapezius muscles. Between the hollow below the tuberosity of the occipital bone at the back of the head and the mastoid process. Locate close to the base of the skull. This point is normally located as the tenderest point of the hollow.

Striking: Strike straight in to the point or slightly upward into the point towards the center of the head for stronger results.

Observed effects of strike. A light strike can cause a severe headache, and a stronger strike will cause dizziness and senselessness or knockout.

Known effects: A knockout with a difficult recovery.

Theoretical effects: A very strong strike may cause brain damage and even death.

Explanation: The place of this point is apt to be attacked by wind evil and the point is important in treating diseases caused by wind evil.

Primary Actions and Functions: Eliminates wind, Benefits the head and eyes, Clears the sense organs, Activates the channel and alleviates pain and Subdues Liver Yang. Brighten the eyes and sharpens hearing, Harmonizes Ki and blood.

Korean: Poong Jee: Wing Pool or Pond: 풍지

Chinese: Feng Chi: Feng = Wind or wind evil. Chi = Pool. 風池

Japanese: Fuchi

Special Note: If you have a frontal or temporal headache this is a very good point to message to help get rid of the headache.

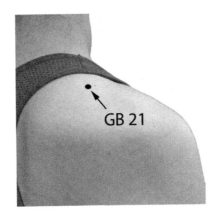

Gall Bladder (GB 21): 견정 : 肩井

Location: On the shoulder, directly above the nipple, at the midpoint of the line connecting Governing 14 and the acromion, at the highest point of the shoulder at the crest of the trapezius muscle. This point is normally located at the point of maximum tenderness.

Striking: Straight down into the point with a hand strike or kick. This point is also used for pressing and grabbing techniques.

Observed effects of strike. This point causes great pain and with a strong press, grip, or strike can cause the individual to drop straight to the ground.

Known effects: Strong enough pressure or striking may cause lightheadedness and dizziness.

Theoretical effects: A very strong strike may cause a knockout.

Special Note for Application: This point is contraindicated during pregnancy. Do not strike press or otherwise apply direct pressure to this point during pregnancy. Although unlikely it is possible that this point could induce premature labor in pregnant women.

Explanation: This point is in the middle of the shoulder, in the depression that looks like a well.

Primary Actions and Functions: Relaxes sinews, promotes lactation and promotes labor. Regulates Ki, activates the channel and alleviates pain. Transforms and lowers phlegm and dissipates nodules.

Korean: Gyun Jung: Shoulder Well: 견정

Chinese: Jian Jing: Jian = Shoulder. Jing = Well 肩井

Japanese: Kensei

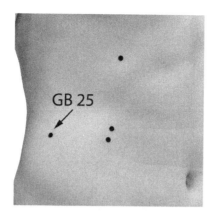

Gall Bladder (GB 25): 경문 : 京門

Location: On the lateral side of the abdomen, on the lower border of the free end of the 12th rib, anterior (front) and inferior (below) to the free end of the 12th rib.

Location Note: To locate the free end of the twelfth rib, first place the entire hand on the upper abdomen and with gentle finger pressure palpate (feel) downwards along the costal margin (bottom of rib cage), until the end of the eleventh rib is located just above the level of the umbilicus. Then palpate further along the inferior margin of the ribcage until the free end of the twelfth rib is located in the lateral lumbar region.

Striking: Straight in from the side of the body with a hand strike or kick.

Observed effects of strike. Great pain in the kidney area, and getting the wind knocked out. Cracked rib.

Known effects: Tip end of rib broken off requiring surgery to repair. Blood in the urine from a damaged kidney.

Theoretical effects: A very powerful strike can cause death from severe kidney damage or failure.

Explanation: This point is on the side of the chest which is a big mound of human body. It is used to relieve morbid worry and terror.

Primary Actions and Functions: Tonifies the Kidneys and regulates the water passages. Fortifies the Spleen and regulates the intestines. Strengthens the lumbar region.

Korean: Gyung Moon: Capital Gate or Door: 경문

Chinese: Jing Men: Jing = Mound, terror or worry. Men = Gate. 京門

Japanese: Keimon

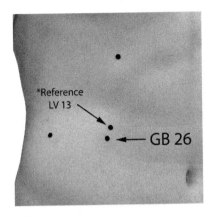

Gall Bladder (GB 26): 대맥 : 帶脈

Location: Directly below Liver 13 (Jang Moon) anterior and inferior to the free end of the eleventh rib, level with the umbilicus.

Location Note: Locate the free end of the eleventh rib (see gall bladder 25) and Liver 13 (Jang Moon), at the crossing point of a vertical line through the free end of the eleventh rib and a horizontal line through the umbilicus. Directly below Liver 13 (Jang Moon).

Striking: Straight in from the side of the body in to the point.

Observed effects of strike. Making the body freeze in its position, unable to move temporarily. Pain and getting the wind knocked out of the individual.

Known effects: A hard enough strike may cause a knockout.

Theoretical effects: A very powerful strike may affect the heart, causing a heart attack and death.

Explanation: The Daimai vein or Girdle Channel passes this point. It is also the place clothes tape is fastened to. It is used to treat morbid leucorrhoea.

Primary Actions and Functions: Regulates the Girdle Vessel and drains dampness. Activates the channel and alleviates pain. Warms Kidney cold, soothes the sinews and regulates menstruation.

Korean: Dae Maek: Girdle Vessel: 대맥

Chinese: Dai Mai: Dai = Tape or morbid leucorrhoea. Mai = Meridian or vein. 帶脈

Japanese: Taimyaku

Gall Bladder (GB 30): 환도 : 環跳

Location: On the postero-lateral aspect of the hip joint, one third of the distance between the prominence of the greater trochanter (hip joint) and the sacro-coccygeal hiatus (where the spine and coccyx meet).

> **Striking:** Straight in from the rear into the hollow of the buttock with a hand strike or kick.
>
> **Striking note:** This point has a lot of muscle protecting it, and must be hit directly and strong to achieve results from the strike.
>
> **Observed effects of strike.** Great pain in the hip area, causing temporary paralysis of hip movement. Pain can increase if not treated properly.
>
> **Known effects:** Damage to the hip joint, possibly severe. Inability to walk.
>
> **Theoretical effects:** Broken hip joint, leg damage, and knockout is possible with a direct, powerful strike.

Explanation: Bending and jumping are two closely related movements. One cannot jump with legs that are curved and cannot stretch. This point is an essential point for the treatment of leg diseases. When this point is to be located, the subject should lie on his side with his thigh flexed and his shank stretched, then a depression is present in the location of the point.

Primary Actions and Functions: Activates the channel and alleviates pain. Benefits the hip joint and leg. Strengthens the lumbus and legs. Dissipates wind-damp in the channels and connecting vessels.

Korean: Hwan Doh: Jumping Circle or Encircling Leap: 환도

Chinese: Huan Tiao: Huan = To bend or curve. Tiao = Jump. 環跳

Japanese: Kancho

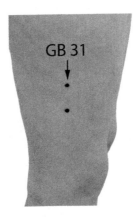

Gall Bladder (GB 31): 풍시 : 風市

Location: On the midline of the lateral aspect of the thigh, 7cun above the transverse popliteal crease.

Location Note: When standing erect with the hands close to the sides, the point is where the tip of the middle finger touches.

Striking: Straight in to the side of the leg with a hand strike, kick, or shin strike.

Observed effects of strike. Great pain in the leg, and with a strong enough strike the leg will become temporarily paralyzed. This is often called "Dead Leg". Can cause the individual to collapse.

Known effects: This point can cause so much pain and confusion that the person does not know what is going on.

Theoretical effects: If the strike is direct enough and strong enough into the point, it is possible to affect the heart by causing it to slow down or even stop.

Explanation: This place is apt to be attacked by wind evils. It is a common point used to disperse wind evils.

Primary Actions and Functions: Eliminates wind, Alleviates itching and activates the channel and alleviates pain. Regulates Ki and blood, Strengthens sinews and bones and dissipates cold.

Korean: Poong Shee: Wind Market: 풍시

Chinese: Feng Shi: Feng = Wind or evil wind. Shi = Market. 風市

Japanese: Fushi

Gall Bladder (GB 32): 중독 : 中瀆

Location: On the lateral aspect of the thigh, 2 cun below Gall Bladder 31 (Poong Shee), 5 cun above the transverse popliteal crease, between muscle vastus lateralis and muscle biceps femoris.

Location Note: When standing erect with the hands close to the sides, the point is 2 cun below where the tip of the middle finger touches.

Striking: Straight in to the side of the leg with a hand strike, kick, or shin kick.

Observed effects of strike. Great pain and "dead leg" (temporary paralysis) from a strong strike. Can cause the individual to collapse.

Known effects: This point can cause so much pain and confusion that the person does not know what's going on. It can also cause nausea.

Theoretical effects: This point can cause knockout if the point is hit hard enough. It may also cause great damage to the knee joint.

Explanation: This point lies in the river-like long depression on the lateral side of the thigh between the two meridians of the Urinary Bladder (foot Taiyang, big yang) and Stomach (foot Yangming, bright yang) channel.

Primary Actions and Functions: Activates the channel and alleviates pain. Soothes sinews, expels wind and dissipates cold.

Korean: Joong Dohk: Middle Ditch: 중독

Chinese: Zhong Du: Zhong = Middle. Du = Big river. 中瀆

Japanese: Chutoku

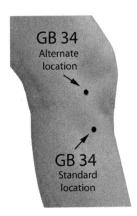

Gall Bladder (GB 34): 양능천 : 陽陵泉

Location: In the tender depression approximately 1 cun anterior and inferior to the head of the fibula.

Location Note: To avoid confusing the head of the fibula with the tibial condyle, slide your fingers up the lateral (outside) aspect of the lower leg until the soft tissue of the musculature gives way to the bony prominence of the head of the fibula.

Alternate Location of this Point: In Korean martial art circles this point is sometimes located directly in the middle of the lateral side of the knee joint in the depression between the tendons.

Striking: Straight in to the point at approximately a 45 degree angle from the front of the leg. Use a hand strike or kick directly into the point. For the alternate location strike straight in to the point at a 90 degree angle to the point.

Observed effects of strike. Great pain temporarily preventing use of the leg. Inabilaity to stand on that leg.

Known effects: Damage to the knee joint with a strong enough strike.

Theoretical effects: May cause knockout with a direct and strong enough strike. This point may cause tendon problems through the body if left untreated.

Explanation: This point is below the projection of the end of the fibula, on the lateral side of the knee. It is opposite of Spleen 9 (Yinlingquan).

Primary Actions and Functions: Benefits the sinews and points, activates the channel and alleviates pain. Promotes the smooth flow of liver Ki. Sooths the sinews and vessels. Clears Gall Bladder damp heat and Relieves stagnation in the channels and connecting vessels.

Korean: Yang Neung Chun: Yang or Sunny Hill Spring: 양능천

Chinese: Yang Ling Quan: Yang = The lateral side of the human body. Ling = Projection. Quan = Spring or fountain. 陽陵泉

Japanese: Yoryosen

THE LIVER CHANNEL

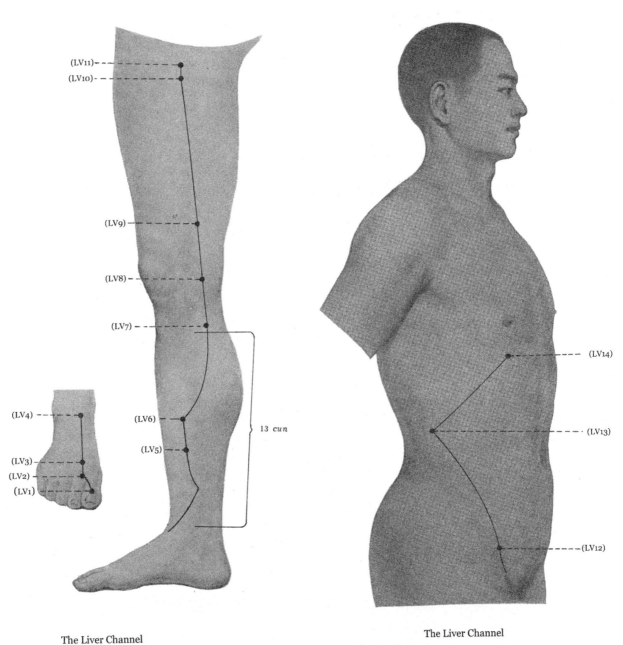

(LV11)

(LV10)

(LV9)

(LV8)

(LV7)

(LV4)

(LV6)

(LV5)

13 cun

(LV3)

(LV2)

(LV1)

(LV14)

(LV13)

(LV12)

The Liver Channel

The Liver Channel

Superficial pathway and measurement on the body

For Liver channel flow and functions see page 191.

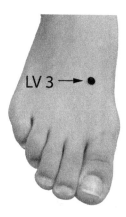

Liver (Lv 3): 태충 : 太沖

Location: On the dorsum (top) of the foot, in the hollow distal to the junction of the first and second metatarsal bones.

Note about this point name: The name of Liver 3 "Tae Choong", Great Rushing, refers to this point's function as the great passageway for the flow of Ki in the channel. It is a primary point for promoting the free flow of Liver Ki. The free flow of Liver Ki is an essential function for good health.

Striking: Straight down into the point with a hand strike or kick. Pressing into the point with a knuckle or object is common.

Observed effects of strike. Great pain and numbing of the foot. Can cause the individual to suddenly collapse.

Known effects: Causing so much pain that the individual cannot stand on the foot.

Theoretical effects: A strong enough strike may break foot bones and cause the individual to feel totally disoriented, confused, and unable to think straight.

Explanation: The combination of the Kidney channel with the Penetrating channel (Chong meridian) is called Taichong. The location of this point is a communications hub of the foot.

Primary Actions and Functions: Subdues Liver yang and extinguishes wind. Spreads Liver Ki and nourishes Liver blood and Liver Um. Clears the head, eyes and regulates the lower burner. Extinguishes Liver fire and clears Liver yang. Pacifies the Liver, regulates blood and opens channels.

Korean: Tae Choong: Great Rushing or Surge or Impact: 태충

Chinese: Tai Chong: Tai = Imperial, highest or greatest. Chong = Communications hub. 太沖

Japanese: Taisho

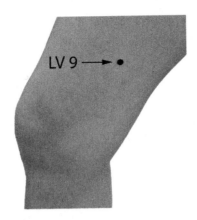

Liver (Lv 9): 음보 : 陰包

Location: Directly superior to the medial epicondyle of the femur, 4 cun, in the cleft between m. vastus medialis and m. Sartorius.

Location Note: Locate one patella's (knee cap) height (2 cun) above the superior border of the patella, in the tender depression between m. vastus medialis and m. Sartorius.

Striking: Strike with hand, knee or leg straight into the point for best results.

Observed effects of strike. Great pain, numbing of the leg or collapsing of the leg with inability to walk.

Known effects: Serious long term injury to the upper leg forcing one to use a cane or crutches to walk.

Theoretical effects: It is possible to be knocked out with a direct and powerful strike on this point. Permanent damage to the body is possible. This point is said to be able to kill a person by causing liver failure.

Explanation: All three foot Um (yin) meridians and all the diseases of the organs in the lower abdomen including uterus diseases are contained in the range of application of this point.

Primary Actions and Functions: Regulates Ki, promotes urination, Adjust menstruation and regulates the lower burner. Adjust the Penetrating and Conception vessels. Clears and disinhibits the Lower Burner.

Korean: Um Bo: Um's wrapping: 음보

Chinese: Yin Bao: Yin = Yin's energy or interior or three foot yin meridians; the lower abdomen. Bao = Wrapping or Contain or Uterus. 陰包

Japanese: Impo

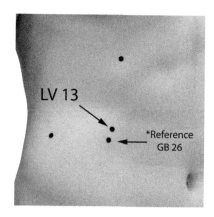

Liver (Lv 13): 장문 : 章門

Location: Directly anterior and inferior to the free end of the eleventh rib.

Location Note: When the arm is bent at the elbow and held against the side, the point is roughly located at the level of the tip of the elbow.

Striking: This point is usually hit straight in from the front. It is possible to hit this point from the side or at an angle coming from the front. A hand strike or kick can be used.

Observed effects of strike. Great pain, being temporarily unable to move, and getting the wind knocked out. Bruised and or broken rib from the strike.

Known effects: Knockout with a very strong strike.

Theoretical effects: On the left side the spleen can be ruptured, and on the right side the liver can be ruptured. This point can cause death.

Explanation: The shape of the ribs looks like a flat topped mountain. The point is below it. The place of this point is covered with clothes and it is a screen protecting the internal organs.

Primary Actions and Functions: Harmonizes the Liver and Spleen, Regulates the middle and lower burner. Spreads the Liver Ki and regulates Ki. Transforms stasis and fortifies the Spleen.

Korean: Jang Moon: System's Door or Completion Gate: 장문

Chinese: Zhang Men: Zhang = Cover, screen or a flat on the mountain. Men = Gate, guard and protect. 章門

Japanese: Shomon

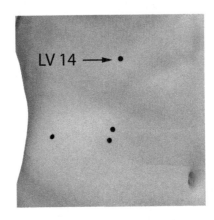

Liver (Lv 14): 기문 : 期門

Location: Directly below the nipple on the mammillary line, in the sixth intercostal space, 4 cun lateral to the midline.

Striking: This point can be hit straight in for the best effect or at a slight angle from outside toward the middle.

Observed effects of strike. Pain, bruising, and getting the wind knocked out.

Known effects: Broken ribs from a strong strike.

Theoretical effects: Knocked out from a strong strike. This point can cause heart problems or lung problems. It is possible to cause death from striking this point.

Explanation: This is a title for a rank of an ancient army officer. Something like commander of the royal guards. Here it is a metaphor referring to the Liver. Liver functions are like a general or an officer. This point is also a gate for the blood and the vital energy that is circulating.

Primary Actions and Functions: Promotes the smooth flow and spreading of Liver Ki and regulates Ki. Invigorates blood, disperses masses and harmonizes the Liver and Stomach. Transforms phlegm and disperses stasis. Calms the Liver and promotes Ki flow.

Korean: Kee Moon: Cycle Gate or Expectation's Door: 기문

Chinese: Qi Men: Qi = Expect or cycle. Men = Gate. 期門

Japanese: Kimon

THE EIGHT EXTRAORDINARY CHANNELS

The Eight Extraordinary (Irregular) Channels: (Meridians)

The eight extraordinary channels are the Governing channel, the Conception channel, the Penetrating channel, the Girdling channel, the Um (Yin) linking channel, the Yang linking channel, the Um (Yin) motility channel and the Yang motility channel. They are thus named because they do not fit the pattern of the major channels. They do not have a continuous, interlinking pattern of circulation, nor or they associated with a specific major organ. They serve as compensating reservoirs, filling and emptying in response to the varying conditions of the major channels and exerting a regulating effect on them, which is why they are given the designation of channel (vessel).

Functions of the eight Extraordinary (Irregular) channels:

*They provide additional interconnections among the twelve regular channels.

*They regulate the flow of Ki and Blood in the twelve regular channels. Surplus Blood and Ki is taken up from the twelve regular channels, and is released when Ki and Blood in the regular channels is empty.

*They are closely related to the liver and the kidney, and some of the minor organs. "The eight extraordinary channels serve the liver and the Kidney".

*They are directly related to the womb, the brain, and other anatomic structures.

Special Note about the Governing and Conception Channel:

The Governing and Conception channel are two of the eight extraordinary channels, but are exceptional among these eight in that they have their own points. For this reason the Governing and Conception channels are often included with the twelve primary channels (and together known as the fourteen channels). The other six extraordinary channels have no points of their own, passing instead through points of the fourteen channels.

The Governing and Conception channels are like midnight and midday; they are the polar axis of the body. There is one source and two branches. One channel goes to the front of the body, and the other channel to the back of the body. When we try to divide these, we see that Um and Yang are inseparable. When we try to see them as one, we see that they are an indivisible whole. Um and Yang must exist together in harmony, otherwise there can be no life or health. Separation of Um and Yang is death.

THE GOVERNING CHANNEL

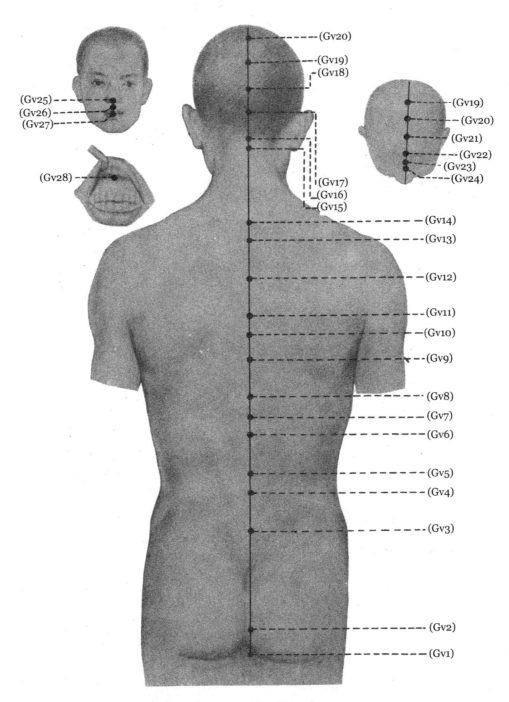

The Governing Vessel

Superficial pathway and measurement on the body

For Governing channel flow and functions see page 192.

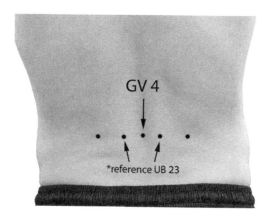

Governing (Gv 4): 명문 : 命門

Location: On the midline of the lower back, in the depression below the spinous process of the second lumbar vertebra.

Location Note: This point is located one intervertebral space above the line connecting the highest points of the two iliac crests (highest point of the hip bones). It is usually located in the deepest spot in the bend of the lower back. Also you can locate the navel with your finger and make a horizontal straight line around the body to locate Governing 4 (Myung Moon).

Striking: Straight in to the point or slightly downwards or upwards with a hand strike or kick.

Observed effects of strike. Great pain so that the individual cannot continue. Knees colasping with a strong downward angle strike.

Known effects: Back pain that continues for days or weeks. Bruising that also causes pain and limits movements.

Theoretical effects: This is a very dangerous point that can cause permanent injury, paralysis, or spinal damage. This point can also cause death.

Explanation: This point lies between the two Urinary Bladder 23 points (Shenshu points). It is of vital importance. It has a lot to do with life and it is the gate through which the energy of life gets in or out. It is the oppsite point to "Ki Hae" Ren 6.

Primary Actions and Functions: Regulates the Governing channel, tonifies the Kidneys and Benefits the lumbar spine. It nourishes the original Ki and warms the gate of vitality. Soothes the sinews and harmonizes blood, builds Kidney Yang and strengthens the Kidneys.

Korean: Myung Moon: Gate of Life or Life's Door: 명문

Chinese: Ming Men: Ming = Live or of vital importance. Men = Gate. 命門

Japanese: Meimon

Special Note: This point is one of the so called "Delayed Death touch" points.

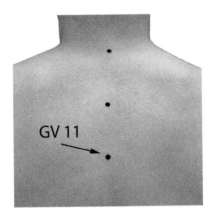

Governing (Gv 11): 신도 : 神道

Location: On the midline of the upper back, in the depression below the spinous process of the fifth thoracic vertebra.

Striking: Straight in to the point or slightly upwards. For maximum effect the scapula (shoulder blades) need to be spread apart or open and not close together.

Observed effects of strike: This point can knock the wind out of you very easily. Or sometimes it is said that it can "take your breath away."

Known effects: This strike is very painful and will damage the spine by bruising or causing even more serious movement problems.

Theoretical effects: This point can cause damage to internal organs especially the heart and lung. This point can cause heart palpitations if hit hard enough. With a very strong strike this point may also cause lung damage. Death is possible with this point.

Explanation: This point is on the same level as Urinary Bladder 15 and is followed by Governing 10. It is the road on which the mind travels in or out. This point is of a very high rank, like the Sun or the Heart.

Primary Actions and Functions: Tonifies the Heart and Lung and it calms the spirit. Pacifies internally generated wind which ascends along the Governing channel. Quiets the Heart and Spirit and relieves pain.

Korean: Shin Doh: Spirit Pathway: 신도

Chinese: Shen Dao: Shen = mind, the state of mind, spirit, or the Yang energy of the body. Dao = Big road, mind or spirit in the chest or heart. 神道

Japanese: Shindo

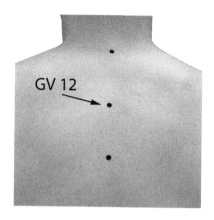

Governing (Gv 12): 신주 : 身柱

Location: On the midline of the upper back, in the depression below the spinous process of the third thoracic vertebra.

Striking: Hit this point straight in or slightly upwards.

Observed effects of strike: This point can knock the wind out. It can also cause neck whiplash if the strike is strong enough. Neck pain may continue without treatment.

Known effects: Bruising to the spine and causing movement problems of the spine.

Theoretical effects: This point can cause serious lung problems like uncontrollable coughing and may cause the body to deteriorate consistently over time.

Explanation: This point is on the pillar of the whole body.

Primary Actions and Functions: Tonifies Lung Ki, strengthens the body and calms spasms. Clears the Heart and calms the spirit. Supports the Lung and Dispels pathogens.

Korean: Shin Joo: Body Pillar: 신주

Chinese: Shen Zhu: Shen = The whole body. Zhu = Pillar. 身柱

Japanese: Shinchu

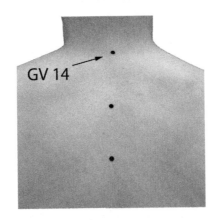

Governing (Gv 14): 대추 : 大椎

Location: On the midline in the depression below the spinous process of the seventh cervical vertebra. It's where the seventh cervical and First thoracic vertebra meet. The big knot of bone at the base of the neck.

Note about the Name: The name "Dae Choo" is also the name of the red date called jujube in English. Governing 14 (Dae Choo) is similar to the red date because when the body gets too hot the point turns red like the red date and is similar in shape. This point also controls heat dissipation in the body. It's interesting to note that when people get hot they cool themselves down with a wet towel around the back of the neck. It is this point they are trying to cover whether they realize it or not. This is an alternate reason the points name is Dae Choo.

Striking: Straight in to the point or upwards or downwards will be effective using a hand strike or a kick.

Observed effects of strike. Pain, bruising, headache, or light-headedness from a soft strike. Knockout from a slightly stronger strike.

Known effects: Disorientation or unconciousness from a medium-hard strike.

Theoretical effects: This point can severely damage the spine causing any number of physical or mental problems. A strong direct strike can also cause death.

Explanation: This point is below the seventh cervical vertebra. That is the biggest of all the vertebras in the spinal column.

Primary Actions and Functions: Clears Heat, Regulates Nutritive and Defensive Ki. Clears the mind and tonifies the yang. Frees Yang Ki of the whole body. Clears the Heart and quiets the spirit.

Korean: Dae Choo: Great or Big Vertebrae (Great Hammer): 대추

Chinese: Da Zhui: Da = Big. Zhui = Vertebra. 大椎

Japanese: Daitsui

Special Note: This point is forbiden to strike in contact sports due to its danger.

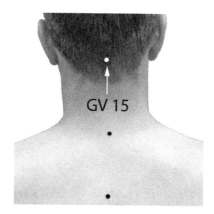

Governing (Gv 15): 아문 : 啞門

Location: This point is located at the base of the posterior skull on the midline 0.5 cun inside the hair line, in the depression below the spinous process of the first cervical vertebra. The first cervical vertebra is usually impalpable.

Special Note about the Name: It is said this point is named "Ah Moon" because when it is hit with enough power (and doesn't knock out the person or if they are recovering from a knockout) the individual cannot talk but can only make the sound of "Ah-Ah-Ah." Thus the name "Ah Moon" the gate of Ah.

Striking: Straight in or slightly upward with a hand strike or kick.

Note about striking: This is one of the most dangerous points on the body for striking.

Observed effects of strike: With a soft strike dizziness, headache and disorientation is common. A little harder strike causes knock out.

Known effects: This point causes muteness. Striking with the right amount pressure will cause the person to only be able to say "Ah," hence the name "Ah" Moon. Also this point will put your brain in a state that can only be described as being "out on your feet."

Theoretical effects: This point causes knockout, muteness, possible deafness, and even schizophrenia. This point also causes death when hit hard and directly.

Explanation: This point is at a very important position. It is used to cure aphasia and it can cause dumbness as well.

Primary Actions and Functions: Benefits the tongue and treats muteness, Clears the mind and stimulates speech. Benefits the neck and spine and Clears the spirit-disposition.

Korean: Ah Moon: Mute's Gate or Gate of Dumbness: 아문

Chinese: Ya Men: Ya = Aphasia or dumb. Men = Gate, key position or important place. 啞門

Japanese: Amon

Special Note: This point is used for the treatment of collapse of Yang characterized by loss of consciousness, aversion to cold, cold counter flow of the limbs, purple lips etc. This is a forbiden point to strike in full contact sports competitions due to its danger.

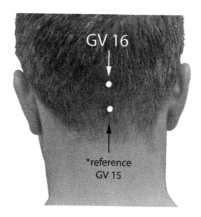

Governing (Gv 16): 풍부 : 風府

Location: One cun directly above the midpoint to the posterior hairline, directly below the external occipital protuberance, in the depression between M. trapezius of both sides.

Location Note: The external occipital protuberance is found as the bony prominence at the base of the skull on the midline, though in some individuals it may be difficult to feel. This point lie's approximately 1 cun above the posterior hairline.

Striking: Straight in using a hand strike or kick. A slightly upwards strike is very effective also.

Note about Striking: This is one of the most dangerous points on the body to strike.

Observed effects of strike. A soft strike can cause pain, headache, dizziness and disorientation.

Known effects: A medium hard strike can cause a knockout.

Theoretical effects: A hard strike can cause mental disorders and affect sensory organs like smell, hearing, and vision. A strong strike will cause death.

Explanation: The back of the head and neck is most liable to be invaded by wind evil, along with the points on this part of the body. Governing 16 (Fengfu) is one of those points. It is one of the points that is essential in the treatment of diseases caused by wind evil.

Primary Actions and Functions: Eliminates wind, Clears the mind and Benefits the brain. Clears spirit disposition, Frees the joints and drains fire and Dissipates cold.

Korean: Poong Boo: Palace of Wind or Wind's Dwelling: 풍부

Chinese: Feng Fu: Feng = Wind or evil wind. Fu = Storehouse. 風府

Japanese: Fufu

Special Note: This is a forbiden point to strike in contact spotrts due to its danger.

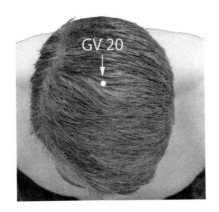

Governing (Gv20): 백회 : 百會

Location: At the vertex on the midline, in the depression 5 cun posterior to the anterior hairline and 7 cun superior to the posterior hairline. It is located at the apex of the head.

Alternate Names for Governing 20: The first is, "Three Yang Five Meetings", because Governing 20 is the meeting point of the governing vessel with the three yang channels of the Urinary Bladder, Gall Bladder and Triple Burner, as well as the Liver channel. The second is "Mud Ball Palace" which refers to the material aspect of the spirit which is located in the brain and accordingly Governing 20 is sometimes considered to be the location of the upper DahnJun (cinnabar field). Next the name "Mountain of Heaven", reflects its location at the highest point of the body. The name "Ghost Gate" reflects its influence on psycho-emotional disorders.

Striking: Straight down onto the point with a hand strike or kick.

Observed effects of strike. Pain, headache, and disorientation with a medium hard strike.

Known effects: A hard strike can cause a knockout.

Theoretical effects: A very hard strike can cause shock, and if the strike has enough power this point can cause death.

Explanation: This point is on top of the head, at the highest place. All parts of the body and all the channels pay respects to it or worship it like stars paying respects to the polestar.

Primary Actions and Functions: Clears the mind, lifts the spirits, tonifies Yang and promotes resuscitation. Lifts fallen Yang Ki, discharges blazing heat in the yang channels. Benefits the brain and calms the spirit and nourishes the sea of marrow.

Korean: Baek Hae: Hundred Meetings or Convergences: 백회

Chinese: Bai Hui: Bai = Hundred or all. Hui = Meet, pay respects to or worship. 百會

Japanese: Hyakue

Special Note: Governing 20 is located at the apex of the head, the highest and hence most yang point of the body. It therefore has a profound effect on regulating Yang, both to descend excess Yang and to raise deficient Yang.

Special Note for Meditation: The effect of raising Yang is emphasized in Ki Gong (Ki Breathing) practice. Attention is focused on the upper DahnJun, either Governing 20 or Extra point Um (Yin) Tang, located between the eyebrows, in case of sinking of Ki, aversion to wind and cold in the head, hypotension etc., but contraindicated in cases of excessive Yang, fire or wind.

Heaven, Earth and Man are the three powers. Governing 20 (Baek Hae) echoes Heaven, Conception 21 (Sun Ki) echoes man and Kidney 1 (Yong Chun) echoes the Earth. It is by opening Governing 20 that we can better absorb the energy of heaven, and through focusing on Kidney 1 that we root to the energy of the earth. It is strongly emphasized, however, that since Yang has a natural tendency to rise to the head, most people should first master sinking the Ki to the lower DahnJun, located in the lower abdomen, or to Kidney 1, and circulating the Ki through the small heavenly circuit (the Governing and Conception vessels) before focusing unduly on the upper DahnJun.

It is my experience that some people or groups that practice meditation do not practice the Lower abdomen breathing first. They just begin meditation. That often leads to the Yang Ki rising to excess. That can cause many problems including physical or mental problems. It is not uncommon to see mental anomalies in people that don't practice the lower abdomen Ki breathing. In martial arts the lower abdomen breathing is always more important than any other type of breathing.

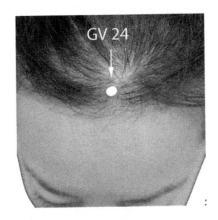

Governing (Gv 24): 신정 : 神庭

Location: On the midline, 0.5 cun within the midpoint of the ideal anterior hairline. If the hairline is indistinct locate this point 5 cun anterior to Governing 20.

Striking: Strike straight in to the upper forehead or straight down on the point with a hand strike or kick.

Observed effects of strike: With a strong strike, headache, confusion, or being "out on your feet."

Known effects: A very strong strike can produce a knockout.

Theoretical effects: A very powerful strike directly on the point can cause brain damage or even death.

Special Note for Application: If a person is "out on their feet" lightly shocking this point with a palm strike or some similar strike will bring the person back to sharp focus.

Explanation: This point lies in a noble place. It is the palace of the vitality of the brain.

Primary Actions and Functions: Benefits the brain and calms the spirit. Benefits the nose and eyes. Discharges heat and opens the portals. Eliminates wind and benefits the head.

Korean: Shin Jung: Courtyard of the Spirit or Spirit Yard: 신정

Chinese: Shen Ting: Shen = Vitality of the brain. Ting = Palace. 神庭

Japanese: Shintei

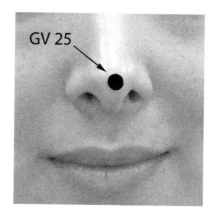

Governing (Gv 25): 소료 : 素髎

Location: In the midpoint of the tip of the nose.

Striking: Straight in to the tip of the nose with a hand strike or kick.

Observed effects of strike: A soft strike causes tears and blurred vision. A medium strike causes the nose to bleed, and a harder strike causes a broken nose or knockout.

Known effects: A strong strike can cause shock.

Theoretical effects: To dispel a myth, you cannot drive the nose bone into the brain with an upwards palm strike: the nose "bone" is actually soft cartilage and will not penetrate the skull.

Special Note for Application: Recent research has shown this point to be effective in restoring loss of consciousness. As a revival technique you must strongly stimulate the tip of the nose to help revive someone that has loss of consciousness.

Explanation: This point is on the tip of the nose. It is not a wide place, but it is very noble. Sitting straight and looking at the nose tip with half closed eyes, one can get a white shadow or outline of the nose.

Primary Actions and Functions: Benefits the Nose. Discharges heat and opens the portals and returns Yang.

Korean: Soh Ryo: White Bone-Hole, White Crevice or Plain Seam: 소료

Chinese: Su Liao: Su = White color or noble and unsullied. Liao = Bone crevice or deep hole adjacent to the bone. 素髎

Japanese: Soryo

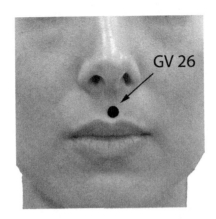

Governing (Gv 26):인중 : 人中

Location: Above the upper lip on the midline, at the junction of the upper third and lower two thirds of the philtrum. The philtrum is the marked indentation found on the midline between the root of the nose and the margin of the upper lip.

Special Location Note: The name of this point (Man's Middle) reflects the location of this point close to the junction of the Governing and Conception vessels, and between the nose and mouth.

Striking: Straight in to the point with a hand strike or kick. This point can also be used for grabbing and eagle claw techniques.

Observed effects of strike: Pain and tears with a soft strike or strong eagle claw grip.

Known effects: With a hard strike shock or knock out can occur depending on the power of the strike.

Theoretical effects: A strike with enough power can cause death.

Special Note for Application: Governing 26 (In Joong) is indicated for resuscitation, and it is the single most important point to revive consciousness and re-establish Um (yin) Yang harmony. In any kind of fainting or loss of consciousness, including knockout, Governing 26 (In Joong) may be strongly pressed or stimulated (obliquely upwards towards the root of the nose) to recover consciousness.

Explanation: This point is under the nose in the ditch near the nostrils. The nasal mucus goes out through this place first. This point is used to treat water disease such as edema.

Primary Actions and Functions: Restores consciousness and clams the spirit. Benefits the face and nose and expels wind. Benefits the spine and treats acute lumbar sprain. Clears the spirit-disposition and Dispersed heat in the interior.

Korean: In Joong: Man's Middle or Water Trough: 인중

Chinese: Shui Gou: Shui = Liquid or nasal mucus. Gou = Ditch. 人中

Japanese: Suiko

Special Note: The Governing vessel which governs all the Yang channels, and the nose which receives Heavenly Ki, both correspond to heaven (Yang). The Conception vessel which governs all the Um channels, and the mouth which receives earthly sustenance, both correspond to Earth (Um). According to Asian cosmology "Man" lies between heaven and earth, and Governing 26 (In Joong) is considered to establish a connection between the two. When the harmonious interaction of Um and Yang is lost and they begin to separate, there is loss of consciousness, with death being the ultimate manifestation of this separation of Um and Yang.

THE CONCEPTION CHANNEL

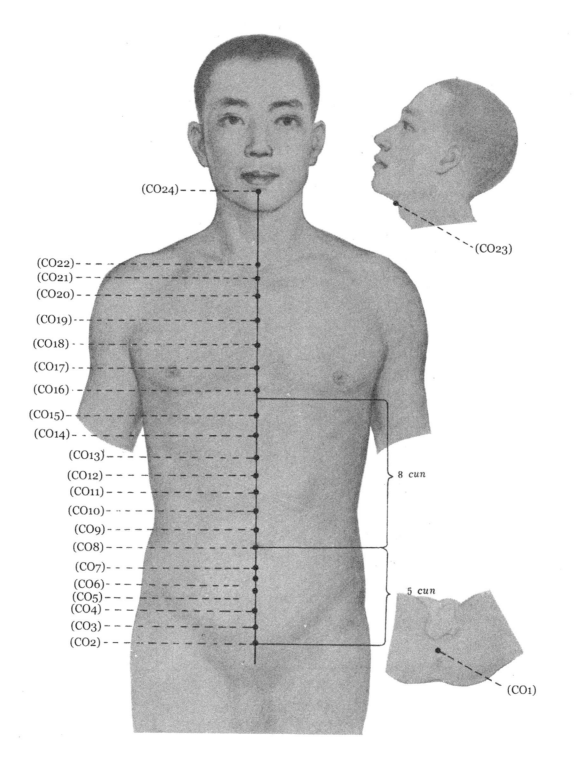

The Conception Vessel

Superficial pathway and measurement on the body

For Conception channel flow and functions see page 193.

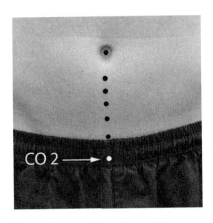

Conception (Co 2): 곡골 : 曲骨

Location: On the midline of the lower abdomen, at the superior border of the pubic symphysis, 5 cun below the umbilicus.

Striking: Straight in or slightly downward into the point with a hand strike or kick.

Observed effects of strike: Pain and knock down with bruising. Getting the wind knocked out.

Known effects: Fracture of the symphysis pubis bone.

Theoretical effects: This point can cause knockout, and a powerful enough strike can cause death.

Explanation: This point and the bone share the same name.

Primary Actions and Functions: Warms and invigorates the Kidneys and Regulates the Lower Burner. Warms the Yang and supplements the Kidneys.

Korean: Gok Gohl: Curved or Crooked Bone: 곡골

Chinese: Qu Gu: Qugu = An ancient anatomical term for pubis. 曲骨

Japanese: Kyokkotsu

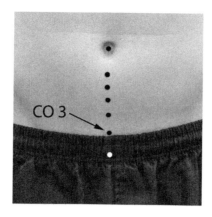

Conception (Co 3): 중극 : 中極

Location: On the midline of the lower abdomen, 4 cun inferior to the umbilicus and 1 cun superior to the pubic symphysis bone.

Striking: Straight in or slightly upwards with a hand strike or kick.

Observed effects of strike: Pain and getting knocked down from a direct strike.

Known effects: Getting the wind knocked out with a strong enough strike. Blood in the urine from damage caused to this point.

Theoretical effects: It is possible to severely damage the bladder striking this point, and it is possible to cause death.

Explanation: Zhongji is another name for the polestar. This point is in the middle or center of the body like the polestar in the sky. It is the root or base of the vital energy of the human body. It is used to treat diseases such as having an urge to empty urine but cannot.

Primary Actions and Functions: Clears Heat, Resolves damp-heat and promotes the Urinary Bladder function of Ki transformation. Warms the palace of essence and Dispels stagnation and benefits the Lower Burner.

Korean: Joong Geuk: Middle Extreme or Central Pole: 중극

Chinese: Zhong Ji: Zhong = Middle, in the middle of the human body or the root or base. Ji = Moat, extreme, position or direction or an urge (to do something). 中極

Japanese: Chukyoku

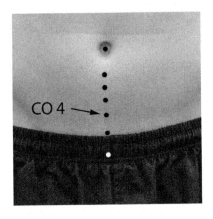

Conception (Co 4): 관원 : 關元

Location: On the midline of the lower abdomen, 3 cun inferior to the umbilicus and 2 cun superior to the pubic symphysis.

Striking: Straight in, slightly downward or slightly upward with a hand strike or kick.

Observed effects of strike: Pain and getting knocked down.

Known effects: Getting the wind knocked out with a strong strike.

Theoretical effects: With a very powerful direct strike it is possible to cause a knockout or even death.

Explanation: This point is in the place in which the vital Um energy and Yang energy of the lower Burner is kept and through which that energy gets in or out.

Primary Actions and Functions: Nourishes blood and Um, Strengthens Yang, Benefits the original Ki, Tonifies the Kidneys, Calms the mind and Roots the ethereal soul. Restores collapse, Supplements Ki and secures the Yang. Warms and regulates the blood chamber and palace of essence and dispels cold damp. Safeguards health and prevents disease.

Korean: Gwan Won: Gate of Origin or Pass of Source: 관원

Chinese: Guan Yuan: Guan = To Keep, store, close or mechanism. Yuan = Vital energy, vitality or vigor. 關元

Japanese: Kangen

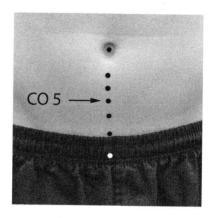

Conception (Co 5): 석문 : 石門

Location: On the midline of the lower abdomen, 2 cun inferior to the umbilicus and 3 cun superior to the pubic symphysis.

Striking: Straight in, slightly upward or slightly downward with a hand strike or kick.

Observed effects of strike: With a medium hard strike one is knocked down.

Known effects: A hard strike can knock the wind out.

Theoretical effects: A powerful and direct strike can cause internal problems and death.

Explanation: A woman with a hypoplastic vagina is called a stone female, who cannot bear a child. This point can cause a woman to be sterile. This point is used to treat a disease called stone abdomen. Suffering from this disease, the patient's (either male or female) lower abdomen is as hard as stone.

Primary Actions and Functions: Strengthens the Original Ki, promotes the transformation and excretion of fluids in the Lower Bruner and opens water passages. Warms Kidneys and invigorates Yang. Alleviates pain.

Korean: Suhk Moon: Stone Gate: 석문

Chinese: Shi Men: Shi = A stone that is hard and no grain can grow on it.

Men = Gate. 石門

Japanese: Sekimon

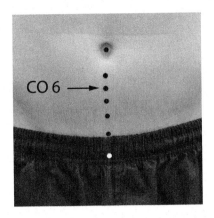

Conception (Co 6): 기해 : 氣海

Location: On the midline of the lower abdomen, 1.5 cun inferior to the umbilicus and 3.5 cun superior to the pubic symphysis.

Special Note about the Name: This point is called Ki Hae which means the Ocean of Ki because the body's Ki is centered and stored here creating the body's "Ocean of Ki."

Striking: Straight in or slightly downward or upward with a hand strike or kick.

Observed effects of strike: Pain and getting knocked down.

Known effects: Getting the wind knocked out.

Theoretical effects: It is possible to cause internal damage and death if the strike is powerful enough.

Explanation: The place of this point is a sea of vital energy or vigor of the human body. It is useful in treating various diseases concerning the vital energy of the human body and the rushing up of distension gas.

Primary Actions and Functions: Tonifies Ki and Yang, Regulates Ki, Tonifies original Ki and resolves dampness. Regulates Ki, harmonizes blood and boosts the origin. Warms the Lower Burner and strengthens deficient Kidneys.

Korean: Ki Hae: Sea of Ki or Ocean of Ki: 기해

Chinese: Qi Hai: Qi = The vital energy in the human body. Hai = Sea or vast and deep. 氣海

Japanese: Kikai

Special note: This point is considered the anatomical center of gravity of the human body. It is also the focus point when meditation is centered on building and storing the Ki in the lower abdomen for use in the body. This is considered to be one of the so called "delayed death touch points".

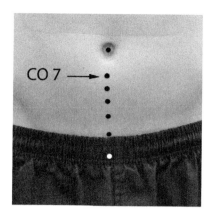

Conception (Co 7): 음교 : 陰交

Location: On the midline of the lower abdomen, 1 cun inferior to the umbilicus and 4 cun superior to the pubic symphysis.

Striking: Straight in, slightly upward or downward with a hand strike or kick.

Observed effects of strike: Getting knocked down due to weak knees.

Known effects: Getting the wind knocked out.

Theoretical effects: Getting knocked out. If the strike is powerful enough it can cause internal damage and even death.

Explanation: This point lies below navel where energies from the upper part and the lower part of human body meet or cross. Besides, it is the meeting place of three meridians, the Kidney, Conception and Penetrating channels.

Primary Actions and Functions: Nourishes Um, regulates the uterus and is a point of the Penetrating Vessel (channel). Warms and supplements Kidney Yang. Benefits the lower abdomen and genital region.

Korean: Um Kyo: Um Junction or Um Intersection: 음교

Chinese: Yin Jiao: Yin = The opposite of Yang or Yin (Um) channels. Jiao = To meet, cross or contact. 陰交

Japanese: Inko

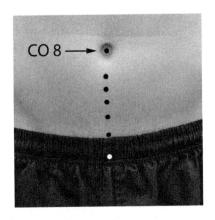

Conception (Co 8): 신궐 : 神闕

Location: In the center of the umbilicus (navel).

Striking: Straight in with a hand strike or kick.

Observed effects of strike: Pain and getting knocked down. Getting the wind knocked out of the individual.

Known effects: Getting knocked out with a direct strike.

Theoretical effects: A direct and powerful strike can cause great internal damage and death.

Explanation: This point is the gate through which vitality gets in or out. It is also the palace in which vitality dwells.

Primary Actions and Functions: Rescues Yang, Strengthens the Spleen and tonifies original Ki. Opens the portals and restores consciousness. Moves gastrointestinal Ki and transforms cold-damp accumulating stagnations.

Korean: Shin Gwuhl: Spirit Gateway (middle of navel): 신궐

Chinese: Shen Que: Shen = Human vitality or navel vitality. Que = Palace, gate or big gap. 神闕

Japanese: Shinketsu

Special Note: This point is forbiden to insert acupuncture needles.

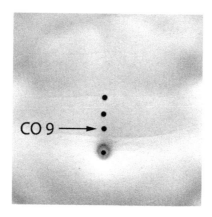

Conception (Co 9): 수분 : 水分

Location: On the midline of the abdomen, 1 cun above the umbilicus and 7 cun below the sternocostal angle.

Striking: Straight in to the point with a hand strike or kick.

Observed effects of strike: Pain and getting knocked down.

Known effects: Getting the wind knocked out.

Theoretical effects: Striking with great power can cause lung, spleen, or kidney damage that may need medical treatment.

Explanation: This point lies over small intestine. It helps small intestine separate the clear from the turbid. The clear water is then conveyed to the bladder and the turbid dregs are conveyed to the large intestine. It is very effective in treating water diseases, that is, diseases caused by inability to separate the clear from the turbid such as diarrhea and dysentery.

Primary Actions and Functions: Promotes the transformation of fluids and controls the water passages. Moves Spleen (earth) and opens water-damp. Harmonizes the intestines and dispels accumulation.

Korean: Soo Boon: Water Separation: 수분

Chinese: Shui Fen: Shui = Water or liquid. Fen = Separate. 水分

Japanese: Suibun

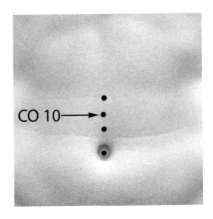

CO 10→

Conception (Co 10): 하완 : 下脘

Location: On the midline of the abdomen, 2 cun above the umbilicus and 6 cun below the sternocostal angle.

Striking: Straight in to the point with a hand strike or kick.

Observed effects of strike: Getting knocked down and getting the wind knocked out.

Known effects: Getting knocked out with a very strong strike.

Theoretical effects: It the strike is direct and powerful enough it is possible to cause death.

Explanation: This point is over the lower part of the stomach.

Primary Actions and Functions: Promotes the descending of Stomach Ki, relieves stagnation of food and tonifies the Spleen. Assists movement and transformation in the Stomach and intestines and disperses digestive accumulations and Ki stagnation.

Korean: Ha Wan: Lower Epigastrium or Cavity: 하완

Chinese: Xia Wan: Xia = Lower. Wan = Stomach. 下脘

Japanese: Gekan

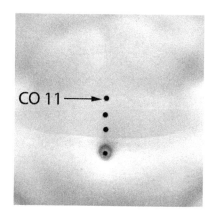

Conception (Co 11): 건리 : 建里

Location: On the midline of the abdomen, 3 cun above the umbilicus and 5 cun below the sternocostal angle.

Striking: Straight in to the point with a hand strike or kick.

Observed effects of strike: Pain and getting the wind knock out. Getting knocked out.

Known effects: Can cause stomach problems with a very strong strike.

Theoretical effects: It is possible to cause great internal damage requiring medical intervention.

Explanation: Water and grain running downstream have to pass through the place of this point then into the stomach. Thus it helps to set up the inner energy of the middle burner and make the internal organs strong and healthy.

Primary Actions and Functions: Promotes the rotting and ripening in the Stomach and stimulates the descending of Stomach Ki. Regulates Ki. Transforms damp and harmonizes the Middle Burner. Moves the Spleen and rectifies Ki.

Korean: Ghun Rhee: Strengthen the Interior or Establish Measure: 건리

Chinese: Jian Li: Jian = Set up, strong and healthy or downstream. Li = Inside. 建里

Japanese: Kenri

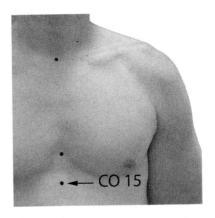

Conception (Co 15): 구미 : 鳩尾

Location: On the midline of the abdomen, 7 cun above the umbilicus and 1 cun below the level of the sternocostal angle.

Location Note: Many sources locate this point below the xiphoid process. In practice however, the xiphoid process varies considerably in length, and this point may lie on the xiphoid process itself. Use the sternocostal angle for the most accurate location.

Special Note about the Name: The name of Conception 15, "Turtledove Tail", reflects the shape of the xiphoid process, likened to the tail of a dove, with the ribs forming the wings.

Striking: Straight in or slightly upward with a hand strike or kick.

Observed effects of strike: Great pain and getting the wind knocked out. Getting knocked out.

Known effects: With a strong enough strike the xiphoid process can be cracked or broken causing serious damage that may need medical intervention to repair.

Theoretical effects: With a very strong strike it is possible to cause death.

Explanation: This point is on the tail of the turtledove, the xiphoid process. The stem of the sternum is the bird's head and the ribs form the two wings. Turtledoves never hiccup, they are also a remedy for the hiccups. This point can be used to treat hiccup, nausea, etc. Its function is similar to that of the turtledove.

Primary Actions and Functions: Calms the mind and benefits the Original Ki. Regulates the Heart and calms the spirit. Descends Lung Ki and unbinds the chest. Clears heat and extinguishes wind.

Korean: Goo Mee: Turtledove Tail: 구미

Chinese: Jiu Wei: Jiu = Turtledove. Wei = Tail. 鳩尾

Japanese: Kyubi

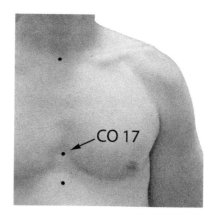

Conception (Co 17): 단중 : 膻中

Location: On the midline of the sternum, in a depression level with the junction of the fourth intercostal space and the sternum. This point can be located directly between the nipples in men.

Striking: Straight in or slightly downward to the point using a hand strike or kick.

Observed effects of strike: Pain, bruising, knocking the wind out and cracking the sternum.

Known effects: Getting knocked out from a very strong strike.

Theoretical effects: This point can cause a heart attack if the strike is powerful enough or at the correct moment of breathing and may cause death.

Explanation: This point is an ancient name for pericardium. This point lies in the middle of the chest. It is necessary to bare the chest before using the point.

Primary Actions and Functions: Tonifies Ki, Regulates Ki, Clears the Lung and benefits the diaphragm and the breasts. Regulates Ki and unbinds the chest. Clears the Lung and transforms phlegm.

Korean: Dahn Joong: Chest Center or Between the Breast: 단중

Alternant Korean name: Jung Joong: Penetrating Order:

Chinese: Dan Zhong: Dan = Bare. Zhong = Middle of the chest or middle. 膻中

Japanese: Danchu

Special Note: This point is considered to be the location of the center of the ancestral Ki.

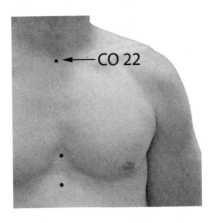

Conception (Co 22): 천돌 : 天突

Location: On the midline, in the center of the suprasternal fossa, 0.5 cun superior to the suprasternal notch.

Striking: Straight in to the point with a hand strike. It is difficult to strike such an enclosed area with a kick. This point is also used with pressing and grabbing technique. Choking is also used with this point.

Observed effects of strike: Pain and gagging with a soft strike or grab. Loss of consciousness due to choking.

Known effects: Bruising and damage to the pressure point area.

Theoretical effects: Knockout with a strong strike, and death with a very powerful strike.

Explanation: Air gets into or out of the lung through the throat. The throat is like a chimney. This point is on the chimney, also called the sky chimney.

Primary Actions and Functions: Benefits the throat and voice. Stimulates the descending of Lung Ki and clears heat. Diffuses the Lung and transforms phlegm.

Korean: Chun Dohl: Heaven's Prominence or Celestial Chimney: 천돌

Chinese: Tian Tu: Tian = Sky, atmosphere or the upper part of the human body. Tu = Chimney. 天突

Japanese: Tentotsu

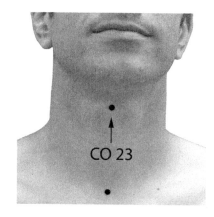

Conception (Co 23): 염천 : 廉泉

Location: On the anterior midline of the neck, in the depression above the hyoid bone (Adam's apple).

Striking: Straight in to the point or slightly upwards with a hand strike. The enclosed area of this point makes it difficult to use a kick. This point is also used with pressing and grabbing technique. Choking technique can also be applied.

Observed effects of strike: Pain and gagging from a soft strike or grab. Choking and unable to breathe temporarily to the point of passing out.

Known effects: Soreness, pain, and bruising to the Adam's apple.

Theoretical effects: With a strong strike enough physical damage may occur to the area causing the person to suffocate to death.

Explanation: This point is on the edge of the Adam's apple. It is the source of the spring of saliva.

Primary Actions and Functions: Dispels interior wind, promotes speech and subdues rebellious Ki. Disinhibits the throat and eliminates phlegm and clears fire.

Korean: Yum Chun: Corner or Ridge Spring or Modesty Spring: 염천

Chinese: Lian Quan: Lian = Side, border, margin or the narrow part. Quan = Spring or fountain. 廉泉

Japanese: Rensen

EXTRA POINTS AND STRIKING AREAS

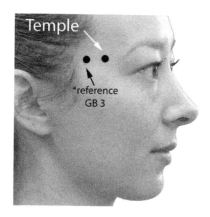

Temple: Dae Yang 대양: 中文: 太阳

Location: This is the temple point. It is located in the depression approximately .5 cun dorsal to the outer corner of the eye

---

Striking: Straight in to the point for the maximum effect. Also striking at an angle will produce strong results as well. This point can also be gripped causing great pain and even disorientation or knockout if the grip is powerful enough.

Observed effects of strike: Great pain, Headache, confusion, and disorientation, and knockout.

Known effects: Damage to the bone structure in the local area.

Theoretical effects: This point can cause instant death with a strong enough strike.

Korean: Dae Yang: Big Yang: 대양

Chinese: Tai Yang: 中文: 太阳

Special Note: This point is well known for being hit with a baseball before baseball helmets were used. There were some deaths from striking this vital point.

Groin: Sah-Tah-Koo-Ni: 사타구니: 中文：腹股ㄏ

Location: This is the area located between the legs in the pubic area.

Striking: Straight in or upward at an angle to the groin with a kick or hand strike. Grabbing techniques are also very effective in this area.

Observed effects of strike: Great pain, incapacitation, and inability to function. Blood in the urine from a medium-strong strike. Permanent injury can be caused from a medium to strong strike.

Known effects: A strong enough strike can produce a knockout.

Theoretical effects: A very strong groin strike is said to be able to cause death.

Korean: Sah-Tah-Koo-Ni: 사타구니

Chinese: Fu gu gou: 腹股ㄏ

Special Note: The Groin area in men is extremely sensitive even with a mild strike. Although probably not as sensitive as in men, what most people don't realize is that this is also a sensitive area for women and can also cause great pain and damage to a women with a strong strike.

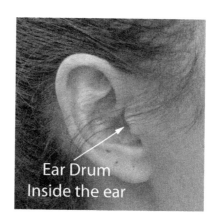

Ear Drum
Inside the ear

Ear Drums: Kwee-Chung or Ko-Mahk 귀청: 고막: 中文 : 鼓膜

Location: Inside the ears.

Striking: Any hand strike or kick will work, but a cupped hand strike covering the ear is the preferred strike.

Observed effects of strike: Great pain, dizziness, and disorientation. Perforated (punctured) eardrum.

Known effects: Temporary loss of hearing. Bleeding from the eardrum. Striking this area can cause unconsciousness.

Theoretical effects: Permanent hearing loss from eardrum damage. If the strike is strong enough death can occur.

Korean: Kwee-Chung or Ko-Mahk: 귀청 : 고막

Chinese: Gu Mo: 中文 : 鼓膜

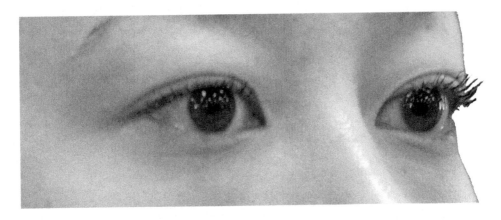

Eyes: Nuen: 눈 : 中文: 目

Location: On the face just below the forehead.

Strike: Any straight in hand strike or kick will be effective however, a finger strike directly to the eyeballs will provide the best results. Angle strikes will also prove effective.

Observed effects of strike: Tearing of the eyes, inability to see temporarily, and broken blood vessels in the eyes. A strike may cause a knockout.

Known effects: Temporary blindness for days or even weeks, depending on the damage to the eyes.

Theoretical effects: Permanent blindness caused by damage from a strike. It is possible to cause death with an eye strike.

Korean: Nuen: Eye: 눈

Chinese: Mu: 中文：目

Under the Tongue point: Hyuh Hyul: 혀혈: 中文： 舌

Location: Under the tongue on top of the lower palate:

Strike: Due to the location of this point grabbing technique is the main method to use on this point.

Observed effects: Great pain, tearing of the eyes, inability to close the jaw or bite down on the finger pressing the point. Weakness in the knees and legs.

Known effects: Unable to stand until pressure released.

Theoretical effects: It is possible to create fainting with enough pressure.

Korean: Hyuh Hyul: Tongue: 혀혈:

Chinese: She: 中文： 舌

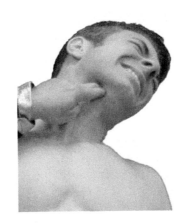

Under the Chin point: Ah-Gu Hyul: 아구혈 : 中文: 上廉泉

Location: Directly under the chin of the lower jaw in the soft part lateral to the midline approximately .5 cun next to the lower jaw bone. Approximately in line with points Stomach 5 and or Stomach 6.

Strike: This point is usually hit with a smaller striking surface such as fingers or one knuckle strike. The striking direction is upwards and angle slightly inwards towards the middle of the skull. This point is also used for pressing and grabbing to take down or control an opponent.

Observed effects of strike: Extreme pain, tearing of eyes, weakness in the knees and legs.

Known effects: Knockout from a strong strike.

Theoretical effects: If the strike is strong enough death is possible.

Korean: Ah-Gu Hyul: 아구혈

Chinese: Shang Nian Quan: 中文： 上廉泉

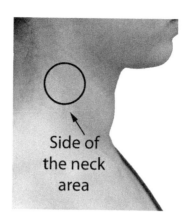

Side of the neck area

Side of Neck Point: Hohn Soo Hyul: 혼수혈 中文: 洪音穴

Location: Directly on the mid frontal plane of the body in the middle of the side of the neck. This spot is a striking area on the side of the neck.

> **Strike:** This point is usually hit with a knife hand, palm or back palm strike, or ridge hand strike. The forearm is also a very effective striking technique.
>
> **Observed effects of strike:** Dizziness, headache, temporary loss of vision, knockout.
>
> **Known effects of strike:** Prolonged unconsciousness.
>
> **Theoretical effects:** Coma and death.

Korean: Hohn Soo Hyul: 혼수혈:

Chinese: Hong Yin Xue: 中文: 洪音穴

Special Note: In the news in 2014 a cricket player was hit with a cricket ball in the side of the neck where Hohn Soo Hyul is located. Days later the cricket player died from that strike to Hohn Soo Hyul. Martial art strikes to many of the pressure points in this book can be just as deadly when accurate and powerful.

PRESSURE POINT OVERVIEW

SECTIONS
OF THE BODY

POINTS LOCATED ON THE HEAD AND NECK

Large Intestine 17: Large Intestine 18: Large Intestine 20: Stomach 1: Stomach 2: Stomach 4: Stomach 5: Stomach 6: Stomach 7: Stomach 9: Stomach 10; Stomach 11: Small Intestine 16: Small Intestine 17: Urinary Bladder 10: Triple Bruner 17: Triple Burner 20: Gall Bladder 3: Gall Bladder 20: Governing 15: Governing 16: Governing 20: Governing 24: Governing 25: Governing 26: Conception 22: Conception 23:

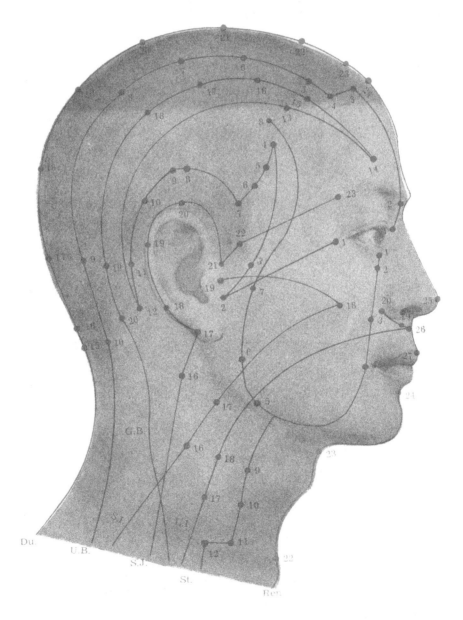

POINTS LOCATED ON THE TORSO

Front:

Lung 1: Lung 2: Large Intestine 16: Stomach 12: Stomach 18: Spleen 12: Spleen 21: Pericardium 1: Gall Bladder 26: Liver 13: Liver 14: Conception 2: Conception 3: Conception 4: Conception 5: Conception 6: Conception 7: Conception 8: Conception 9: Conception 10: Conception 11: Conception 15: Conception 17: Conception 22: Conception 23:

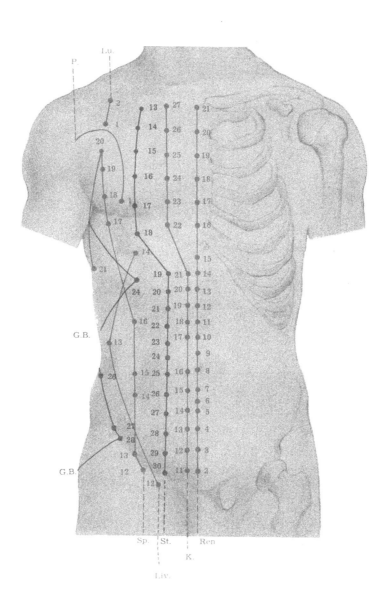

177

Back:

Small Intestine 9: Small Intestine 10: Small Intestine 11: Urinary Bladder 23: Urinary Bladder 42: Urinary Bladder 44: Urinary Bladder 46: Urinary Bladder 47: Urinary Bladder 52: Gall Bladder 21: Gall Bladder 25: Governing 4: Governing 11: Governing 12: Governing 14:

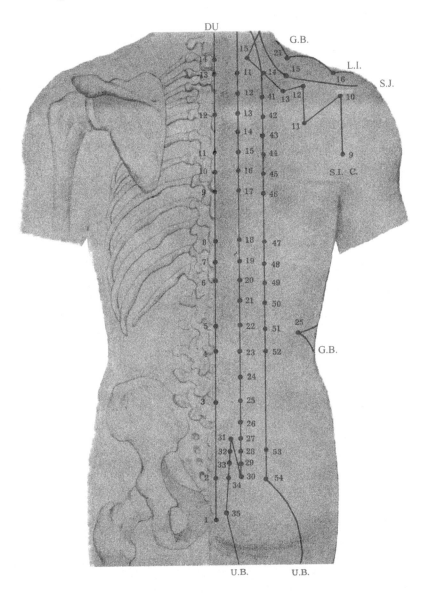

POINTS LOCATED ON THE ARMS AND HANDS

Lung 3: Lung 5: Lung 7: Large Intestine 4: Large Intestine 5: Large Intestine 10: Large Intestine 11: Large Intestine 14: Heart 1: Heart 3: Heart 4: Heart 5: Heart 6: Heart 7: Small Intestine 8: Pericardium 3: Pericardium 6: Pericardium 8: Triple Burner 10:

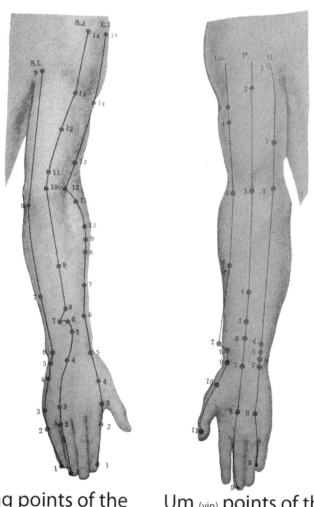

Yang points of the
arm and hand

Um (yin) points of the
arm and hand

POINTS LOCATED ON THE LEGS AND FEET

Stomach 32: Stomach 33: Stomach 35: Stomach 36: Stomach 42: Stomach 43: Spleen 6: Spleen 10: Liver 3, Liver 9: Urinary Bladder 39: Urinary Bladder 40: Urinary Bladder 57: Urinary Bladder 62: Kidney 1: Kidney 10: Gall Bladder 30: Gall Bladder 31: Gall Bladder 32: Gall Bladder 34:

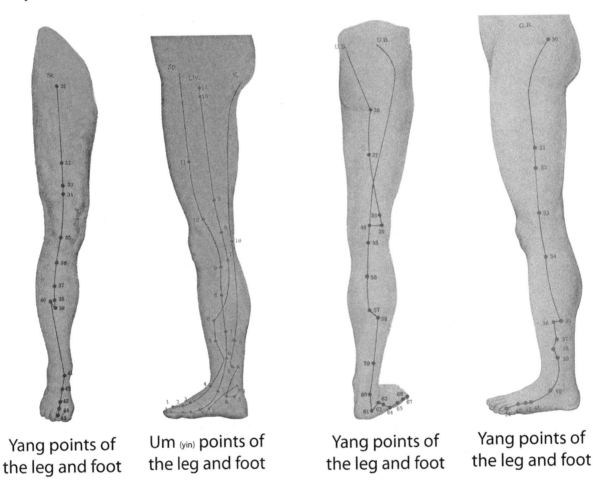

Yang points of the leg and foot

Um (yin) points of the leg and foot

Yang points of the leg and foot

Yang points of the leg and foot

CHANNEL (MERIDIAN) THEORY

There are many legends about the origins of the Channels, Pressure Points, and Acupuncture. There are two legends that are relevant to this book. The first legend is that acupuncture and its related channels and pressure points were discovered by observing soldiers who were wounded by arrows and spears and recovered from a previous ailment (which was unassociated with the arrow and spear wounds) that were in other parts of the body. Trial and error over many centuries evolved into a refined and detailed clinical methodology based on this system of correspondences. The second legend says that semi-divine sages mapped the pathways of Ki and chronicled the effects of ingesting herbs. What was invisible to the ordinary eye was visible to their enlightened perception, the result of enlightened meditation.

There are two main theories that have been advanced to explain the discovery of the channels and pressure points. The first theory says that centuries of observation of the existence of tender spots on the body during the course of disease, and the alleviation of symptoms when they were stimulated by massage or heat, led to the gradual discovery of the pressure points. When sufficient points were known, they were linked into groups with common characteristic and effects, and aided by the observation of propagated sensation when they were stimulated; from that, understanding of channel pathways followed. The second theory says that propagated sensation during the course of massage and more especially the exploration of the internal landscape of the body through meditation and Ki Gong (Ki breathing) practice, led to the discovery of the channel pathways, with the knowledge of specific points coming later. This second theory received strong confirmation from the significant discovery of a silk book during the excavation of the Western Han tomb at *Mawangdui,* which describes the pathways of eleven channels but does not refer to any specific points.

Channels or meridians are the energy pathways that guide Ki, Blood, and Fluids throughout the body. The *Canon of Perplexities* states, "The channels move Blood and Ki and ensure the free flow of Um and Yang, so that the body is properly nourished." They are the communication lines between all parts of the organism. The organs, portals, surface skin and body hair, sinews and flesh, bones, and other tissues all rely on communication through the channels, forming an integrated, unified organism. We may think of the channel (meridian) as rivers of energy that flows to every single cell of the body along its specific path. Then think of the pressure points as places where that energy bubbles up to the surface like a spring. Some points are on the surface and some are deeper than the surface. Every energy pathway or channel (meridian) is inter-connected to all other energy pathways throughout the body thus allowing points to affect areas of the body seemingly not connected.

Organ networks communicate with each other via an invisible web of channels transporting Ki and Blood. The Ki courses through the body in perpetual motion similar to water in a riverbed. Like the matrix of waterways that cover the surface of the earth, these channels empty into one another, intersect, and have underground as well as surface streams, connecting the interior with the exterior. Ultimately the channels connect every single cell of the body with the body's energetic system.

The study of the channels in traditional Asian medicine can be said to be the equivalent of the study of anatomy in Western medicine. Listed below is the order of circulation of the Ki and blood in the twelve regular channels and the time that the Ki flows strongest through the channel. Ki flows in waves and not in straight lines. In nature the only straight line is "Death".

1. The Lung Channel 3am to 5am → 2. The Large Intestine Channel 5am to 7am → 3. The Stomach Channel 7am to 9am → 4. The Spleen Channel 9am to 11am 5. The Heart Channel 11am to 1pm → 6. The Small Intestine Channel 1pm to 3pm → 7. The Urinary Bladder Channel 3pm to 5pm → 8. The Kidney Channel 5pm to 7pm → 9. The Pericardium Channel 7pm to 9pm 10. The Triple Burner Channel 9pm to11pm 11. The Gall Bladder Channel 11pm to 1am 12. The Liver Channel 1am to 3pm

The balanced flow of energy through all the channels creates and maintains good health and strength throughout the body. Any imbalance in the energy flow will cause illness in the system or systems affected. Hence, balance in anything we do is very important for good health and best results.

Lung Channel (Meridian) (Lu)

Arm Greater Um (Yin) Lung Channel (Meridian)

Soo Tae Um Pyea Gyung: 수태음 폐경 手太阴肺经

There are 11 points in the surface pathway of the lung channel.

The inner pathway begins in the region of the stomach in the central Triple Bruner Meridian (Sahm Cho Gyung) and descends the spine in order to connect with the large intestine. The return pathway passes through the cardiac orifice of the stomach and traverses the diaphragm. Then, the channel penetrates the lung, the organ that belongs to it. After the pathway ascends the trachea and connects with the larynx and the pharynx, the channel leaves the chest cavity beneath the clavicle at point Lung 1.

Functions of the Lung:
* Governing Ki and controlling respiration.
* Controlling disseminating and descending function.
* Regulating the water passages.
* Controlling the skin and body hair.
* The Lung opens into the nose.

Large Intestine Channel (Meridian) (LI)

Arm Yang Bright Large Intestine Channel (Meridian)

Soo Yang Myung Dae Jahng Gyung: 수양명 대장경 手阳明大肠经

There are 20 points in the surface pathway of the large intestine channel.

This channel begins at the radial side of the tip of the index finger, passes through the interspace between the first and second metacarpal bones, through the anatomical snuffbox and over the superior part of the lateral aspect of the forearm, to the lateral aspect of the elbow. The shoulder is reached via the lower part of the lateral aspect of the upper arm. From this point the channel branches behind the acromion to the seventh cervical vertebra (Gv 14) and from there runs on to the supraclavicular fossa. From the seventh cervical vertebra (Gv 14) the channel runs through the supraclavicular fossa and enters the ribs where it there connects with the lung. After traversing the diaphragm the channel reaches its organ, the large intestine.

Functions of the Large Intestine:
* The main function of the Large Intestine channel is to receive waste material sent down from the Small Intestine, also to absorb its fluid content and form the remainder into feces to be excreted.
* The Large Intestine is also assisting the Lung in its function of opening the water passages.

Stomach Chanel (Meridian) (St)

Leg Yang Bright Stomach Channel (Meridian)

Johk Yang Myung Wee Gyung: 족양명 위경 足阳明胃经

There are 45 points in the surface pathway of the Stomach Channel.

The surface pathway starts at the lateral side of the nostril and ascends the nose to the inner medial canthus, where it meets the bladder channel. From here the channel runs to its first point on the lower edge of the eye socket and then perpendicular to the corner of the mouth. From this section of the channel branches provide for the gums of the upper jaw, circle the lips, and then meet the Extraordinary Vessel, Conception meridian (Governing or Conception) in the groove of the chin.

From the corner of the mouth the channel descends to the lower jaw and as a facial branch to the corner of the jaw, from where it ascends via the zygomatic arch to the level of the temples and the region of the "Head's Bending" (Stomach 8) in front of the ear. A branch runs to Governing vessel (Dohk Maek or Du Mai) 24.

The main pathway of the channel extends from the lower jaw over the side of the neck and carotid artery to the upper clavicular fossa. Here the channel starts its inner pathway, which runs down from the diaphragm to its organ, the stomach and the spleen. Connections with the deeper layers of the points Conception 12 and Conception 13 are located here.

From the upper clavicular fossa the surface pathway of the channel runs over the chest and nipple to the abdomen, where the channel runs to the side of the straight abdominal muscle and past the umbilicus to the groin. From here the channel continues to run superficially over the antero-lateral aspect of the upper thigh to the side of the patella and then via the anterior aspect of the lower leg and foot dorsum, terminating at the lateral side of the second toenail.

From point Stomach 36 below the knee a branch descends via the antero-lateral aspect of the lower leg and the foot dorsum to the lateral side of the third toe. From point Stomach 42 a branch meets with the spleen channel on the big toe.

Functions of the Stomach:
   * The functions of the Stomach channel are to control the "rotting and ripening" of food, to control descending and to act as the first stage in the digestion of fluids.
   * The Stomach channel is the only yang channel to run along the anterior of the body. For this reason it is considered to be particularly full of Yang Ki.
   * Other functions of the Stomach include regulating the function of the intestines, tonifying Ki, Blood, Um and Yang.

Spleen Channel (Meridian) (Sp)

Foot Tae (Greater) Um (Yin) Channel (Meridian)

Johk Tae Um Bee Gyuhng: 족태음 비경 足太阴脾经

There are 21 points on the surface pathway of the spleen channel.

The channel begins at the inside (medial) corner of the nail of the big toe and ascends in its surface pathway from here via the instep, at the border between the sole and dorsum, in front of the medial malleolus (ankle bone), to the lower leg. From the lower leg the channel then runs along the posterior (back) border of the tibia and crosses below the knee in front of the liver channel. On the upper leg it runs over the antero-medial (front inside) aspect of the inner thigh.

Above the groin the channel enters in its inner pathway into the deeper layers of the points Conception 3 and 4. It then reaches points Spleen 14 and Spleen 15 on the surface. From this stage the channel runs to the inner layers of point Conception 10 and then its inner branch runs through the abdomen to its organ, the spleen, where it connects with the stomach. It ascends further via the diaphragm to the heart and connects with the heart channel.

The surface pathway of the channel in the abdomen leads initially from the deep layers at point Conception 10 back to point Spleen 16, to the side of the upper abdomen. From here the channel follows, via points Gall Bladder 24 and Liver 14, along the side of the chest to points Spleen 17 to Spleen 20.

At point Spleen 20 in the 2ⁿᵈ ICS (inter-costal space; between the ribs) an inner branch leads via the deeper layers of point Lung 1 along the throat to the root of the tongue and disperses in the region of the tongue base. From point Spleen 20 to the channel rises again into the 6ᵗʰ ICS (some books say the 7ᵗʰ ICS), below the armpit, to point Spleen 21.This is where the "Great Spleen Network Vessel" begins.

A branch breaks off in the area of the stomach, crossing the diaphragm to transport Ki to the heart.

Functions of the Spleen:

The Spleen has five principal functions.

* The first is dominating the transportation and transformation of the liquid and solid products of digestion after they have been "rotted and ripened" by the Stomach. It therefore plays a major role in the digestive process, the production of Ki and blood, the function of the intestines and the proper discharge of fluid.
* The second is controlling the blood, dominating the first stage of its formation and holding it in its proper place and preventing hemorrhage (bleeding).
* The third is dominating the muscles and the four limbs, providing vigor and bulk.
* The fourth is opening into the mouth and dominating the sense of taste.
* The fifth is controlling the raising of Ki to counteract sinking and prolapse.

Heart Channel (Meridian) (Ht)

Arm Lesser Um (Yin) Heart Channel (Meridian)

Soo Soh Um Shim Gyuhng: 수소음 심경 手少阴心经

There are 9 points in the surface pathway of the Heart channel.

The inner channel pathway originates at the heart and the "heart-system", with all its connections to the other organs. The descending part of the channel traverses the diaphragm to connect with the small intestine. The ascending part ascends alongside the esophagus, connects with the root of the tongue, and to the "eye system", i.e. the eyeball and accompanying tissues. The main pathway of the channel runs through the lung and leaves the chest cavity from the side in the axilla, at point Heart 1.

The surface pathway comes from the axilla and runs, firstly, to the medial aspect of the inner upper arm, the inside of the elbow joint and finally to the antero-medial aspect of the inside of the lower arm. In the region of the wrist joint the channel runs radially past the pisiform bone, then via the palm of the hand to the radial corner of the nail of the little finger.

Functions of the Heart:
* The Heart has five principal functions:
* The first is governing the blood and blood vessels.
* The second is housing the "Spirit", also called the "Mind". This is the belief that a person's spirit is centered and kept in the heart and not in the brain or head.
* The third is the heart opens into the tongue.
* The fourth is that the heart governs sweating.
* The fifth is the heart condition manifest itself in the individual's complexion.

The Small Intestine Channel (Meridian) (SI)

Arm Greater Yang Small Intestine Channel (Meridian)

Soo Tae Yang Soh Jahng Gyuhng: 수태양 소장경 手太阳小肠经

There are 19 points in the surface pathway of the small intestine channel.

The small intestine primary channel originates at the ulnar corner of the nail of the little finger. It ascends in its surface pathway, over the outside aspect of the little finger and the hand at the dividing line between the skin of the dorsum and the palm, to the region of the wrist. The channel then ascends, via the ulnar region of the outside of the lower arm, the Canalis nervi ulnaris, and the posterior aspect of the upper arm, to the posterior aspect of the shoulder joint. It zigzags over the scapula and branches to connect with the seventh cervical vertebra (Du 14).

From here the inner pathway of the channel descends through the superior fossa of the clavicle and connects with the heart. It further descends alongside the esophagus through the diaphragm, reaching the stomach, and finally connects with its organ, the small intestine.

The surface pathway runs from the superior clavicular fossa, alongside the neck and over the lower jaw to the cheekbone (SI 18), branching to the inner corner of the eye (Bl 1) and then connecting with the bladder channel. Before reaching point Si 18, a branch runs from the cheek to the outer corner of the eye (GB 1), before finally entering the ear at point SI 19.

Functions of the Small Intestine:
* The principal function of the Small Intestine organ is to receive, transform and separate fluids, the only indications relating to this function are dark and hesitant urination (SI 2 Jun Gohk and SI 3 Hoo Gyea).
* Even more notably, despite the fact that the channel connects with the diaphragm and Stomach, passes through Ren 12 Joong Wan and Ren 13 Sang Wan, and descends to the Small Intestine.
* No points of the Small Intestine channel are indicated for disorders of the digestive system.

Urinary Bladder Channel (Meridian) (UB)

Leg Greater Yang Urinary Bladder Channel (Meridian)

Jok Tae Yang Bang Gwang Gyung: 족태양 방광경 , 足太阳膀胱经

There are 67 points on the surface pathway of the Urinary Bladder Channel, also called the Bladder Channel.

In its surface pathway the channel originates at the inner canthus of the eye and ascends along the forehead to the Dong Maek (Governing Channel) on the anterior hairline (Gv 24). From here the channel runs laterally to points UB 3 and UB 4 and further over the skull. At the vertex the channel runs from UB 7 to the Governing channel Gv 20 and then to UB 8. From the vertex branches enter the brain, in the direction of the tip of the ear at point GB 8. From point UB 9 the channel returns to the Governing channel (Gv16) and then descends to point UB 10. After crossing the skull the channel separates at point UB 10 into its two principal branches along the spine. These run almost parallel to the midline.

The first branch runs over the seventh cervical vertebra (Gv 14) and first thoracic vertebra (Gv 13), from where it descends along the spine at 1.5 cun lateral to the midline to the region of the sacrum, at the level of the fourth sacral foramen (hole). The channel then returns cranially toward the midline where it descends from the first sacral vertebra, via the sacral foramen, to the center of the buttocks and finally, via the center of the posterior aspect of the thigh, to the popliteal fossa at UB 40.

In the lumbar region (UB 23 and UB 52) the inner channel pathway branches via the lumbar muscles into the interior, where it connects with the kidney and its organ, the Urinary Bladder.

The surface pathway of the second branch descends from point UB 10 and paravertebrally from the second thoracic vertebra, but at 3 cun from the midline, along the inner border of the scapula to the lumbar-sacral region (UB 54). From here it descends further over the buttocks (GB 30) and the posterior aspect of the thigh to the popliteal fossa (UB 40).

Both channel branches meet at point UB 40 in the popliteal fossa and descend via the middle of the calf along the Achilles tendon to the heel. The channel circles the outer bones from behind and follows the fifth metatarsal bone on the border between dorsum and sole, to end at the outer nail corner of the little toe.

Functions of the Urinary Bladder Channel:
* The function of the Urinary Bladder channel is to store fluid and via its Ki transformation action to convert the waste into urine for excretion. Like the Small and Large Intestine and Triple Burner (Sam Cho) Channels, However, there is little direct clinical relationship between the Urinary Bladder channel and the functions of the Bladder organ.
* Due to its length and the different regions of the body it traverses, points of the Urinary Bladder channel have a great range of actions and indications.

Kidney Channel (Meridian) Ki

Leg Lesser Um (Yin) Kidney Channel (Meridian)

Johk Soh Um Shin Gyung: 족소음 신경 , 足少阴肾经

There are 27 points on the surface pathway of the kidney channel.

The surface pathway of the channel originates at the underside of the little toe and ascends to point Ki 1 on the sole of the foot. From here, the channel traverses the arch of the foot to the navicular bone and the region inferior to the bone on the instep of the foot. The channel then performs a loop, which reaches under the inner bone and ascends again to the posterior part of the inner side of the lower leg in front of the Achilles tendon. However, point Ki 8 is located at the posterior border of the tibia, distal to point Spleen 6 which is also traversed by the Kidney channel. The channel then continues to ascend the leg to the medial side of the popliteal fossa and traverses the posterior aspect of the inner thigh to the region of the public symphysis.

The inner pathway of the channel begins at point Ki 11, ascending over the spine before branching off to connect with its organ, the Kidney and connecting with the Urinary Bladder. Another branch runs from the kidney via the liver and diaphragm to the lung, where it connects with the heart and where other branches in the center of the chest lead to the pericardium channel. From the lung the channel ascends lateral to the larynx and pharynx to terminate at the root of the tongue.

The surface pathway ascends from the pubic symphysis to the lower and upper abdomen, where the channel runs strictly parallel to the midline. It then traverses the chest alongside the midline at a slightly greater distance from the midline to the angle at the chest and clavicle joint. From about point Kidney 25 a branch runs to the heart and lungs.

Functions of the Kidney Channel (meridian):
* The Kidneys have five principal functions.
* The first is storing essence and dominating reproduction, growth and development.
* The second is producing marrow, filling up the brain, dominating bones and assisting in the production of blood.
* The third is dominating water.
* The fourth is controlling the reception of Ki.
* The fifth is opening into the ears and dominating the two lower Um (yin) the anus and the urethra).

Pericardium Channel (Meridan) (P)

Arm absolute Um Pericardium Channel (Meridian)

Soo Gwuhl Um Shim Poh Gyung: 수궐음 심포경 , 手厥阴心包经

There are 9 points on the surface pathway of the pericardium channel.

The inner pathway originates at the chest, where it serves its organ, the pericardium. The channel descends through the diaphragm to the abdomen and then connects with the upper, middle, and lower burner.

The surface pathway emerges from the chest near the nipple at point Pericardium (P) 1. From here the channel ascends to the axilla and follows the antero-medial aspect of the upper arm, via the vessel-nerve street, to the cubital fossa. The channel then ascends further the middle of the antero-medal aspect of the lower arm, between the tendons of the palmaris longus and flexor carpi radialis, to the palm of the hand and the tip to the middle finger.

A branch leads from point Pericardium (P) 8 to the tip of the ring finger and connects with the Triple Burner Channel (Sahm Cho Channel).

Functions of the Pericardium Channel (meridian):
* The main function of the Pericardium channel is, as the wrapping or protector of the Heart, and the disturbance of consciousness manifesting as mental confusion and even coma that occurs during the course of febrile (Hot) diseases as ascribed to the pericardium rather than to the Heart.

The Triple Burner Channel (Meridian) (TB)

Arm Lesser Yang Triple Burner Channel (Meridian)

Soo So Yang Sahm Cho Gyung (han gul)수소양 삼초경 手少阳三焦经

There are 23 points in the surface pathway of the Triple Burner channel.

The surface pathway of the Triple Burner channel originates at the ulnar corner of the nail of the ring finger. From here the channel ascends via the dorsum of the hand between the fourth and fifth metacarpal bones and the central part of the outer aspect of the lower arm between the ulna and the radius, to the tip of the elbow. The channel further ascends via the posterior aspect of the upper arm and reaches the posterior aspect of the shoulder, traversing points of other channels such as Small Intestine 12 and Gall Bladder 21. From Point Gall Bladder 21 the channel runs first to the superior fossa of the clavicle and from here returns to the seventh cervical vertebra (Governing 14).

From the superior fossa of the clavicle the inner pathway of the channel descends to the center of the chest, connects with the pericardium and traverses the diaphragm, thereby connecting all the parts of its organ, the upper, middle, and lower Triple Burner.

From the seventh cervical vertebra (Governing 14) the channel ascends to the region behind the ear. It branches at point Triple Burner 17 directly into the ear and leaves the ear again in front of the ear at point Triple Burner 21. From here it connects with point Triple Burner 23 lateral to the eyebrow and the gall bladder channel lateral to the eye socket in the region of point Gall Bladder 1.

Functions of the Triple Bruner Channel (Meridian):

The Triple Burner channel belongs to the fire phase, is interiorly-exteriorly coupled with the Pericardium channel and is paired with the Gall Bladder channel.

The heat clearing action of the Triple Burner channel points extends to clearing heat from all regions traversed by the channel. This includes the following.

*   Benefiting the ears.
*   Clearing heat from the eyes.
*   Clearing heat from the neck, throat and tongue.
*   Soothing the Heart and calming the spirit.
*   Treating headaches and harmonizing the Triple Burner.

Gall Bladder Channel (Meridian) GB

Leg Lesser Yang Gall Bladder Channel (Meridian)

Jok So Yang Dahm Gyung: 족소양 담경 足少阳胆经

There are 44 points on the surface pathway of the gall bladder channel.

The surface pathway of the channel originates at the bony limit of the outer canthus and runs in front of the ear, before ascending to the region of the temple. From here the channel returns to the anterior part of the helix and passes the ear to the region of the mastoid process. From here the channel again arches over the temples to the forehead, before returning at a slightly more medial level over the scull and reaching the neck region at point gall bladder 20.

A branch from the principal channel departs from below gall bladder 20, just below point gall bladder 12. It then runs through point triple burner 17 through the ear and point small intestine 19 in front of the ear, to gall bladder 1.

A further branch leads from point gall bladder 1 to the lower jaw at point stomach 5, before ascending to the cheek at point small intestine 18 and descending back to point stomach 6 at the corner of the jaw.

From here the branch runs to the superior clavicular fossa, where it reconnects with principal channel from point gall bladder 20.

From the superior clavicular fossa the inner pathway of the channel winds its way ino the chest, traverses the diaphragm, connecting with the liver and entering its organ, the gall bladder. The channel descends further down the flank, where it makes contact with the deep layers of point Liver 13 before entering the superficial layers in the region above the groin and descending past the hip to point gall bladder 30.

The further surface pathway of the channel covers the channel from gall bladder 20 in the region of the neck, via the seventh cervical vertebra (Governing 14), to point gall bladder 21 on the descending aspect of the trapezius muscle, and from here to the upper shoulder region and point small intestine 12 to the superior clavicular fossa. The channel zig-zags over the axillar region to the side of the chest and flank to point gall bladder 29 in the region of the hip. From here, a branch runs to the sacral bone, via point's urinary bladder 31- urinary bladder 34 before reconnecting with the inner branch and the surface pathway of the principal channel at point gall bladder 30. From point gall bladder 30 the channel descends alongside the middle region of the antero-lateral aspect of the thigh, passing the outside of the knee to the middle part of the antero-lateral aspect of the lower leg and in front of the outside ankle bone, via the dorsum, to the outside corner of the nail of the fourth toe.

From point gall bladder 41 on the dorsum of the foot a branch runs between the first and second metatarsal bones to the big toe, where it connects with the liver channel.

Functions of the Gall Bladder Channel (meridian):

The Gall Bladder Channel has two principal functions.
*   The first is to store and excrete bile.
*   The second is to rule courage, decision-making and judgment.

Liver Channel (Meridian) Lv.

Leg Absolute Um Liver Channel (Meridian)

Johk Gwuhl Um Gahn Gyung: 족궐음 간경 足厥阴肝经

There are 14 points on the surface pathway of the Liver channel.

The surface pathway of the channel originates at the outside corner and the base of the nail of the big toe and ascends via the dorsum of the foot, between the first and second metatarsal bones, to the region in front of the inside ankle bone. From here the channel connects with Spleen 6 (Sahm Um Kyo) and ascends via the center of the inside of the shin bone. Below the knee the channel crosses behind the spleen channel and runs inside, past the knee over the central aspect of the inside of the upper leg, to the groin, where it passes over the points Spleen 12 (Choong Moon) and Spleen 13 (Boo Sah) before rounding the external genitalia and the pubic region over the abdomen in the region of the points Conception 3 (Joong Guek) and 4 (Gwahn Won). From here the surface pathway of the channel ascends to the ribcage at point Liver 13 (Jang Moon) and ends at point Liver 14 (Ki Moon) below the nipple.

The internal pathway of the channel originates at point Liver 14 (Ki Moon), where it connects with the liver and gall bladder. A branch traverses the diaphragm and ascends to the lung before descending through the diaphragm again to the epigastrium. Another branch runs cranially alongside the side of the ribcage, touching the larynx and pharynx, and ascends via the cheeks to the "eye system," that is the eyeball with all related structures. From here a branch ascends to the apex, and another descends to the corner of the mouth and circles the lips from within.

Functions of the Liver channel (Meridian):
* The Liver channel has five primary functions.
* The first is the function of storing blood.
* The second is spreading or maintaining the free flow of the Ki.
* The third is dominating the sinews.
* The fourth is opening into the eyes.
* The fifth primary function is manifesting in the nails.

Special Note: The Liver stores blood, the blood is the residence of the Ethereal Soul. When Liver Ki is deficient there is fear. The Liver governs uprising and the Liver dominates physical movement.

Governing Channel (Meridian) Gv

Extraordinary Channel (Vessel)

Dohk Maek Gyung: 독맥 경 督脉

There are 28 points on the surface pathway of the Governing Vessel (Channel).

The surface pathway of the Governing channel originates in the region of the uterus and lower abdomen, where the Conception channel and Chong Mai (extra channel) also originate. In the region of the perineum, a mixture with the Ki of the kidney and bladder channels takes place. On the inside of the spine a branch leads to the kidney and from here ascends further alongside the inside of the spine to the apex, where it enters the brain.

A second branch ascends from the abdomen to the umbilicus and heart. It ascends further, via the region of the throat and pharynx, where contact is made with the Chong Mai and Conception channel, to the lower jaw and inferior border of the eye socket. A further branch ascends from the inner canthus to the apex.

The surface pathway of the channel leads from the perineum region via point Governing 1 at the coccyx and sacrum and the entire spine to the region of the neck. Under the posterior nape of the neck at point

Governing 16 a branch runs to the brain. At the skull, the channel further descends via the midline and nose and philtrum to the frenum of the upper lip.

Functions of the Governing channel:
* The Governing channel is the sea of the Yang channels.
* All six Yang channels converge at the point Governing 14 (Dae Choo).
* The Governing channel has a regulating effect on the Yang channels, so it is said that it governs all the Yang channels of the body.

Conception Channel (Meridian) Co

Extraordinary Channel (Vessel)

Im Maek Gyung: 임맥 경 任脉

There are 24 points on the surface pathway of the Conception Meridian.

The inner pathway of the Conception meridian originates in the pelvic cavity at the uterus and the lower abdomen, where the Governing and Penetrating channel also have their origins. The inner pathway intersects with the Kidney channel and the Governing, and ascends with the other two channels internally alongside the spine. From the source region the Conception channel runs to the perineum region.

The surface pathway of the Conception channel begins at the region of the perineum at point Conception 1. The channel ascends alongside the anterior midline via the lower abdomen, umbilicus, upper abdomen, ensiform process, and sternum to the jugular fossa. The Conception traverses the midline in the region of the trachea and the larynx, where there is contact with the Penetrating Channel, to the chin dimple. Together with the Penetrating channel, branches from the region of the chin encircle the lips and ascend to the area below the eye socket.

Functions of the Conception Channel:
* The conception channel is the sea of the Um channels.
* The three yin channels of the foot all join the conception channel, allowing their bilateral courses to communicate. In this way, the conception channel has a regulating effect on the Um channels, for which reason it is said that it regulates all the Um channels of the body.
* The conception channel regulates menstruation and nurtures the fetus. Thus it is said, "the conception channel governs the fetus".

Special Note about Lower Abdomen Points: The lower abdomen is the location of the DahnJun (cinnabar field), the residence of the deepest energies of the body. Conception 4 and 6 are among the most important tonifying and nourishing points of the body. That is why Ki Gong or Ki Breathing technique is extremely important in martial art training. The energy stored in the DahnJun can be used to enhance one's strength with proper training. For meditation the DahnJun is equally important because it allows the individual to keep centered at all times. Conception 4 is one of the principle points to promote and foster the original Ki, benefit essence, fortify Kidney Yang and nourish Kidney Um. According to classical Asian thought the lower DahnJun, located in the lower abdomen and extending from Conception 7 to Conception 4, is the residence of the deepest energies of the body and the source of all movement.

According the "Classic of Difficulties" The dynamic Ki that moves between the Kidneys is the basis of human life, the source of the organ systems, the root of the twelve channels, the door of respiration and the origin of the Triple Burner. The Taoists believe the DahnJun is the place of the origin of the Original Ki. Due to its location at the heart of the lower DahnJun (cinnabar field) and its close relationship with the original Ki and hence essence, Conception 4 is an indispensable point to tonify and nourish the Kidneys.

As martial artist the lower abdomen or DahnJun is the main area that we try to cultivate during Ki Gong or Ki breathing practice. The goal is to build and store Ki in that area and eventually learn how to use that Ki for martial art and health purposes.

Following are the remaining six extra channels
that have no points of their own.

THE SIX EXTRA CHANNELS

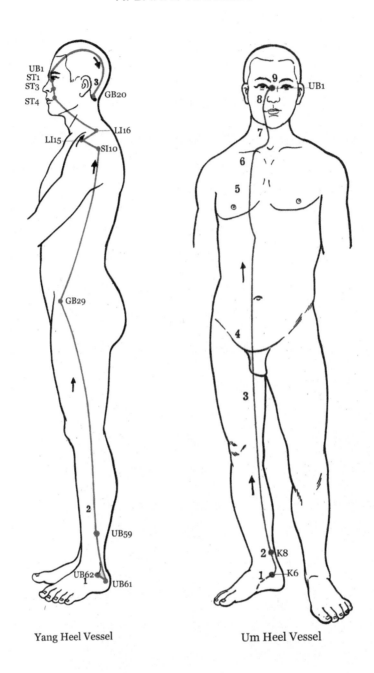

Yang Heel Vessel   Um Heel Vessel

Yang Heel (motility) Channel (Vessel):
Um Heel (motility) Channel (Vessel):

The main physiologic functions of both the Um and Yang motility channels are to control the opening and closing of the eyes, control the ascent of fluids and the descent of Ki, and to regulate muscular activity in general.

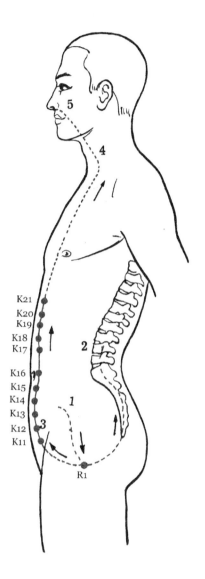

Penetrating Vessel

Penetrating Channel (Vessel):

The penetrating channel is the sea of the major channels. It has a regulating effect on all twelve regular channels, and its main function is to regulate menstruation, for which reason it is also said, "The penetrating channel is the sea of blood."

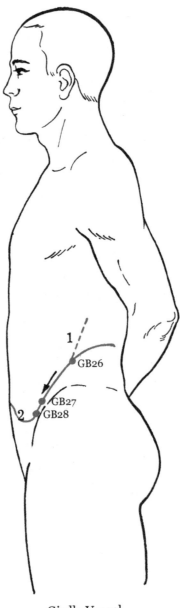

Girdle Vessel

Girdle or Belt Channel (Vessel):

The Girdle channel serves to bind up all the channels running up and down the trunk, thus regulating the balance between upward and downward flow of Ki in the body.

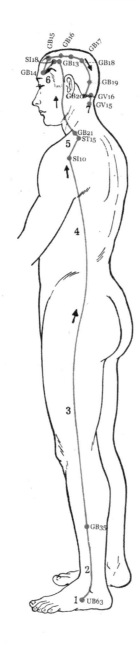

Yang Linking Vessel

Yang Linking Channel (Vessel):

The Yang Linking channel serves to unite all the Yang major channels, strengthening their respective flows, compensating for superabundance or insufficiency in channel circulation, and generally regulating Yang channel activity.

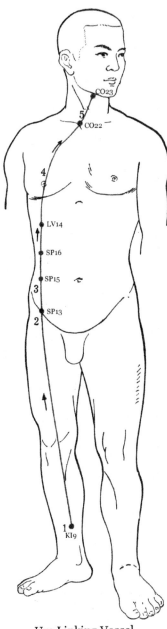

Um Linking Vessel

Um Linking Channel (Vessel):

The Um linking channel serves to connect the flows of the Um major channels, reinforcing and balancing their respective flows, and generally regulating their activity.

200

THEORY OF KI – UM/YANG – FIVE PHASES

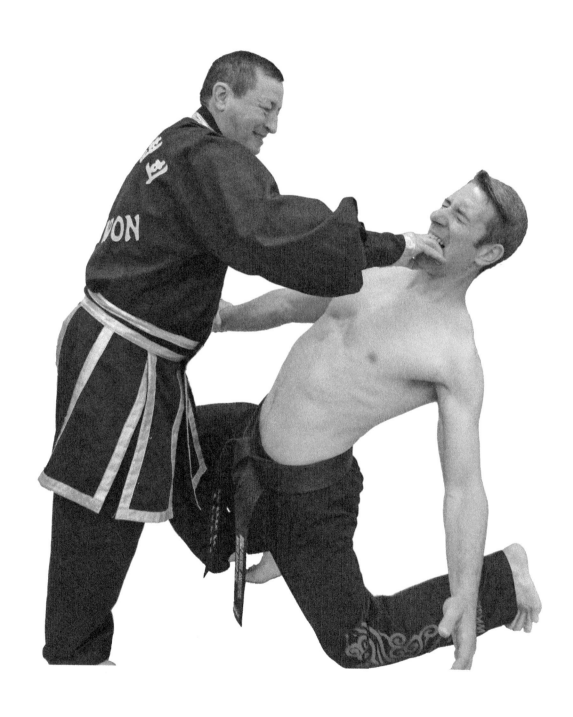

THEORY OF KI (기) (氣)

"Ki" is often translated as universal energy. The Star Wars movies made Ki famous by calling it "The Force." The ancients perceived the existence of Ki and believed it to be the basic element by which all movements and mutations of all phenomena in the universe arise. Ki manifests in many types for specific purposes. Ki changes its form according to its locality and its function. Although all Ki is fundamentally the same, it puts on "different hats" in different places, assuming different functions. For the purpose and understanding of this book, it is not necessary to go into the different types of Ki. However, because of the importance of Ki, I would like to expand on the concept of Ki in Asian philosophy.

The concept of Ki has occupied Asian philosophers of all times, right from the beginning of Asian civilization to our modern times. The original Asian character for Ki indicates that it is something which is, at the same time, both material and immaterial. One part of the character means "vapor," "steam," or "gas." The second part of the character means (uncooked) "rice." This clearly indicates that Ki can be as rarefied and immaterial as vapor and as dense and tangible as rice. It also indicates that Ki is a subtle substance (steam, vapor) deriving from a coarse substance (rice) just as steam is produced when cooking rice.

To actually translate the word "Ki" is very difficult. Many words have been used for translation but none accurately expresses the exact essence of Ki. "Energy," "material force," "matter," "ether," "matter-energy," "vital force," "life force," "vital power," "moving power," and "air" are just a few of the possible translations of the word Ki. One reason it is so difficult to translate Ki is because of its fluid nature; Ki can assume different manifestations and be different things in different situations.

The way Ki is translated also depends on the particular viewpoint taken. Most modern physicists would most likely agree that Ki may be termed "energy" since Ki expresses the continuum of matter and energy as it is now understood by modern particle physics.

Because of the difficulty in finding an appropriate translation for the term "Ki," I will leave it untranslated to allow each person to perceive it as they can best understand the term and all its possibilities.

Ki is the very basis of the universe's infinite manifestations of life, in addition to minerals, vegetables, and animals (including man). It provides continuity between abrasive, material forms, and unsubstantiated, esoteric, non-material energies. The infinite variety of phenomena in the universe is the result of the continuous coming together and dispersion of Ki to form phenomena of various degrees of materialization. The idea of aggregation and dispersion of Ki has been discussed by many Asian philosophers of all times.

Lie Zi, a Daoist philosopher who lived around 300BC said, *"The purer and lighter (elements), tending upwards, made the heaven; the grosser and heavier (elements), tending downwards, made the earth."* Thus "heaven and earth" are often used to symbolize two extreme states of utmost rarefaction and dispersion or utmost condensation and aggregation of Ki respectively.

Huai Nan Zi (c. 122BC), a Daoist book, says: *"Dao originated from Emptiness and Emptiness produced the universe. The universe produced "Ki." That which was clear and light drifted up to become heaven, and that which was heavy and turbid solidified to form earth."*

According to these ancient philosophers, life and death themselves are nothing but an aggregation and dispersal of Ki. Wang Chong (AD 27-97) said, *"Ki produces the human body just as water becomes ice. As water freezes into ice, so Ki coagulates to form the human body. When ice melts, it becomes water. When a person dies, he or she becomes spirit (shin) again. It is called spirit, just as melted ice changes its name to water."* He also said: *"When it came to separation and differentiation, the pure (elements) formed heaven, and the turbid ones formed earth."*

Another philosopher Zhang Zai (AD 1020-1077) further developed the concept of Ki. He proposed that the Great Void was not mere emptiness but Ki in its state of continuity. He said the Great Void cannot but consist of Ki. He also further developed the idea of condensation and dissipation of Ki in giving rise to the myriad phenomena in the universe. He affirmed that extreme aggregation of Ki gives rise to actual form, i.e. material substance. Zhang Zai said, *"The Great Void consists of Ki. Ki condenses to become the myriad things. Things of necessity disintegrate and return to the Great Void."* Also, *"If Ki condenses, its visibility becomes effective and physical form appears."*

It is important to note that Zhang Zai clearly saw the indestructibility of matter-energy. Human life, too, is nothing but a condensation of Ki, and death is a dispersal of Ki. He said, *"Every birth is not a gain, death not a loss. When condensed, Ki becomes a living being, when dispersed, it is the substratum of mutations"*.

In conclusion, we can say that Ki is a continuous form of matter, resulting in physical shape when it condenses and a discontinuous form of matter, resulting in Ki when it disperses. So in classic Asian thought (which often seems contradictory to those not familiar with this form), ***"Ki is and Ki is not."***

THEORY OF UM (YIN) (음 陰) AND YANG (양 陽)

The simplest and most accurate way for me to describe Um (Yin) and Yang is that they are equals but opposites.

The theory of Um-Yang says that every object or phenomenon in the universe consists of two opposite aspects. These opposites are in conflict yet are interdependent. This relationship is the universal law of the material world and the principal and source of the existence of things in the universe. Um-Yang is the root cause of the flourishing and perishing of all things.

The theory of Um-Yang gives us a theoretical model to help us understand the workings of Ki. It helps us understand the opposition, interdepending, inter-consuming or supporting, and the inter-transforming relations of Um and Yang.

By understanding these relationships we can better understand why pressure points work and how they can affect the body through striking and grabbing techniques.

The concepts of Um and Yang and the five phases (elements) were devised by the ancient Asians as a method of defining and explaining the nature of all phenomena. As such they represent the Asian concept of Nature and were fundamental to all natural sciences including medicine, astronomy, calendric science, geography, agriculture, martial art, and warfare. These sciences and philosophies made extensive use of and were strongly influenced by these theories. It is these theories that allow the martial arts and medical arts to overlap in many areas.

The theory of Um and Yang, derived from ages-long observation of nature, describes the way phenomena naturally group in pairs of opposites such as: heaven and earth, sun and moon, night and day, winter and summer, male and female, up and down, inside and outside, movement and stasis. These pairs of opposites are also mutual compliments and interdependent.

The Asian concept of Um and Yang represent opposite by complementary qualities. Each thing or phenomenon could be itself and it's contrary. Therefore, Um contains the seed of Yang, and Yang contains the seed of Um. Every phenomenon in the universe alternates through a cyclical movement of peaks and valleys, and the alternation of Um and Yang is the motive force of its change and development. Day changes into night, summer into winter, growth into decay, and vice versa. Thus the development of all phenomena in the universe is the result of the interplay of two opposite stages, symbolized by Um and Yang. Every phenomenon contains within itself both aspects in different degrees of manifestation. The day belongs to Yang but after reaching its peak at midday, the Um within it gradually begins to unfold and manifest. Thus each phenomenon may belong to a Yang or Um stage but always contains the seed of the opposite stage within itself. Although Um and Yang may appear to be opposite stages, they form a unity and are complementary. One cannot survive without the other. In life the complete separation of Um and Yang is death.

In martial arts the concepts of Um and Yang are generally used to categorize types of movements, anatomic parts, and physiologic functions. For example, fast movement is Yang and slow movement is Um, the back is Yang and the front is Um, the six bowels are Yang and the five viscera are Um, the Ki is Yang and the Blood is Um.

Every phenomenon may be classified as Um or Yang in contrast to another. Each Um or Yang phenomenon itself possesses both Um and Yang aspects that may be further divided in the same way. Within the body the channels that pass over the back and the outer face of the limbs are Yang, while those running through the surface of the abdomen and the inner face of the limbs are Um.

In the tables below are some of the categorizations of body regions, tissues and organs, and physiologic activities.

	Yang (양)	Um (yin) (음)
Parts of the body:	Exterior back, upper body	Interior abdomen, lower body
Tissues and organs:	Surface skin, body hair, bowels	Bones, sinews, viscera
Activity, function:	Ki and defense, agitation, strength	Blood and construction, Calm, weakness

THEORY OF THE FIVE PHASES/ ELEMENTS (오행법) 五元素

This next section on the Five Phases/Elements can enhance our understanding of various interactions that can help with our personal learning process, teaching, and development of students in all areas of martial art training.

The Five Elements are not basic constituents of nature, but five basic processes, qualities, and phases of a cycle or inherent capabilities of change in phenomena. At one time or another, the Five Phase (Element) theory has been applied to martial art strategy and technique, medicine, astrology, the natural sciences, the calendar, music, and politics. A more in-depth study of the five phases can be very useful for any martial artist even today.

Everyone is a mixture of these phases/elements and each tendency will change depending on many things (age, sex, season, learning level, interaction, etc.). Learning to recognize these phases and understand their interaction will benefit your martial art training and your development in Kuk Sool Won™. Following the explanation of the Five Phases/Elements, I will briefly explain how they can help us with our martial art training.

"The Five Phases/Elements are: Water, Fire, Wood, Metal, and Earth. Water moistens downwards, Fire flares upwards, Wood can be bent and straightened, Metal can be molded and can harden, Earth permits sowing, growing, and reaping. That which soaks and descends (Water) is salty, that which blazes upwards (Fire) is bitter, that which can be bent and straightened (Wood) is sour, that which can be molded and become hard (Metal) is pungent, that which permits sowing and reaping (Earth) is sweet."

The Five Phases/Elements also symbolize five different directions of movement of natural phenomena. Wood represents expansive, outward movement in all directions. Metal represents contractive, inward movement. Water represents downward movement. Fire represents upward movement, and Earth represents neutrality or stability.

There are four main cycles of the Five Phase theory. The first is the Creation or Generating Cycle. Then there is the Destruction or Controlling Cycle, then the Influencing Cycle, and finally the Insulting Cycle.

See the figures below to visualize the different cycles:

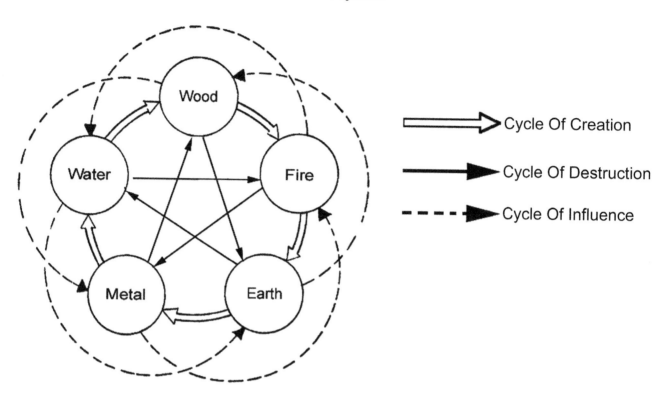

Cycle Of Creation

Cycle Of Destruction

Cycle Of Influence

The Creation, Generating or Inter-promoting relation Phase:

In the generating phase each element generates another and is generated by one. Thus, Wood generates Fire, Fire generates Earth, Earth generates Metal, Metal generates Water, and Water generates Wood.

The Destruction, Controlling or Over-acting and Insulting relation Phase:

In the controlling phase each Element controls another and is controlled by one. Thus, Wood controls Earth, Earth controls Water, Water controls Fire, Fire controls Metal, and Metal controls Wood.

There is also an interrelationship between the Creation or Generating and the Destruction or Controlling sequences. For example, Wood controls Earth, but Earth generates Metal, which controls Wood. Furthermore, on the one hand Wood controls Earth, but on the other hand it generates Fire, which, in turn, generates Earth. Thus a self-regulating balance is kept at all times.

The mutual generating and destruction or controlling relationships among the elements is a fine model of the many self-regulating balancing processes to be seen in nature and in the human body.

The Influence relation Phase:

In this sequence each element Influences another, so that it causes it to decrease. This happens when the balance is broken, and, under the circumstances, the quantitative relationship among the elements breaks down so that, at a particular time, one element is excessive in relation another.

The Insulting relation Phase:

This sequence takes place in the reverse order of the Destruction (controlling) phase. Thus Wood insults Metal, Metal insults Fire, Fire insults Water, Water insults Earth, and Earth insults Wood. This phase takes place when the balance is broken.

The first two sequences deal with the normal balance among the Elements, the second two (the Influencing and the Insulting phase) deal with the abnormal relationships among the Elements that take place when the balance is broken.

Examples of Five Phase Categorization

Category	Wood 木	Fire火	Earth 土	Metal 金	Water 水
Season	Spring	Summer	Late Summer	Autumn	Winter
Climate	Wind	Heat	Damp	Dryness	Cold
Direction	East	South	Center	West	North
Development	Birth	Growth	Maturity	Withdrawal	Dormancy
Color	Cyan	Red	Yellow	White	Black
Taste	Sour	Bitter	Sweet	Pungent	Salty
Viscus	Liver	Heart	Spleen	Lung Large Int.	Kidney
Bowel	Gall Bl.	Small Int.	Stomach	Nose	Urinary Bl.
Sense Organ	Eyes	Tongue	Mouth	Body	Ears
Tissue	Sinews	Vessels	Flesh	Hair	Bones
Disposition	Anger	Joy	Pensiveness	Grief/ Melancholy	Fear/Fright

ABOUT THE AUTHOR

My family is the most important part of my life

After World War II and the Korean War, Asian martial arts began to be shown in America. These early demonstrations began a transformation within the American public that no one could have predicted. That transformation eventually flowed to me and ultimately had a profound impact on my life.

There was a time when I traveled from South Carolina to New York, some 13 hours one way, just to see Chinese martial art movies in Chinatown. I would watch several martial art movies and then drive straight back. Asian martial arts completely dominated my thought and actions.

A year after graduation from high school in 1969, I enlisted in the U.S. Air Force. Little did I suspect that this would lead me to my life's work and my life's love. After completing training as a security policeman, I volunteered for duty in Vietnam. However, instead of being sent to Vietnam, I was sent to Korea. Unknown to me at the time, I was about to begin my life's journey into the Korean culture, history, and martial arts.

I was stationed at the U.S. Air Force base at Kunsan, South Korea. It was there that I was first introduced to the Korean traditional martial art of Kuk Sool by Master Oh, Yi Kuen. For two years I trained in the ancient techniques of this art.

During this period of my training, I was introduced to the use of pressure points, acupressure, Ki (internal energy), herbal medicine, and acupuncture. Master Oh was a 6th degree black belt and the local village healer, and many locals came to him for medical treatment. I also witnessed him treating soldiers that were training in his school. Master Oh treated me with both acupressure and acupuncture for injuries received during fighting. He also gave me herbal medicine for an illness I once had. The treatments were successful and made a deep impression on my psyche. It was my first introduction to Asian pressure points and medicine. It began my interest in pressure point study, herbal medicine, and acupuncture.

I first met Grandmaster Suh, In Hyuk at my black belt testing in Kunsan, Korea. Little did I know what the future held for us. To me, he was my instructor's teacher, a teacher who taught only 4th degree black belts and higher, which, at that time put him way out of my reach. Master Oh was Grandmaster Suh's private student, so Master Oh often invited him to testing's and promotions as a guest of honor.

After my honorable discharge from the Air Force in 1974, I attempted to stay in Korea to study Kuk Sool but was unable to get a visa. I had no choice but to return home to South Carolina. Kuk Sool was not yet taught or practiced in the U.S., so I started a club. That was the only way I could keep in practice and remember the techniques I had learned.

Upon receiving news that Grandmaster Suh had immigrated to the U.S. and was holding a seminar (1975) at Louisiana State University, I jumped on my Harley Davidson and headed out to Baton Rouge to meet him once again. He remembered me from Korea, and, fortunately, with a letter of introduction from Master Oh, he accepted me as his second American student. I began living in his school full time. I was given the Korean martial art name "Suh, Sung Sool" *("Suh" is the family name and "Sung Sool" means to achieve technical skill)* by Grandmaster Suh when he accepted me, and I began a martial art journey from the past that few will ever experience. Many years later I would receive a Korean Buddhist name "Ha, Il Moon" *("Ha" is a family name from the area that Grandmaster Suh is from and "Il Moon" means: first gate).*

My standing orders were to eat, sleep, and train. For five years I lived in Grandmaster Suh's school and followed those orders. At times it was very difficult, and many people told me I was crazy or brainwashed, but I knew that it was a once-in-a-lifetime opportunity. I was determined to make the most of it, no matter how difficult.

While I was living in the school, I saw Grandmaster Suh treat many people with acupressure and acupuncture. I witnessed healing that seemed impossible but happened right in front of my eyes. I also saw Grandmaster Suh use two fingers and put people that came in off the street to challenge him on the ground, screaming in pain. Those events stimulated my interest in learning more about pressure points and how they affect the body. I did not speak Korean well enough to understand Grandmaster Suh's explanations, so I had a difficult time understanding in-depth explanations of pressure points. I did however get both practical experience and the fundamentals of pressure point usage in martial arts thanks to Grandmaster Suh's instruction.

THE POWER OF PRESSURE POINTS

My time living in the school came to an end following my arranged marriage to Lee, Choon Ok, a Korean Kuk Sool Instructor. Our wedding took place July 13, 1980, and we now have two beautiful daughters, Emerald Mi-Yong and Jada Mi-Ho.

In 1981 we opened our first Kuk Sool School in San Mateo, California, and we continue to train under Grandmaster Suh to this day. We have both taught and demonstrated Kuk Sool in many countries around the world, and our martial art education goes on under the watchful eye of Grandmaster Suh.

With the encouragement of my mentor, I started college and earned my B.A. degree from San Francisco State University. Two years later I received my acupuncture degree from the San Francisco College of Acupuncture and Oriental Medicine, providing me with training in healing arts traditionally obtained by high masters. The driving force for me to accomplish these studies was the fact that ancient martial artists were often scholars, and I wanted to follow the ancient tradition. My Kuk Sool mentor, Grandmaster Suh, is one of the best martial artists in the world, but he also knows how to help people through the healing arts of acupressure, acupuncture, and bone setting, as well as herbal medicine. Grandmaster Suh was practicing these techniques many years before these healing arts were recognized in the West and the licensing process begun.

My training with Grandmaster Suh and the study of acupuncture has helped me understand the mystery of pressure points and how they work. As with most subjects, the more you learn the more you realize there is to learn. Even though I am a licensed acupuncturist since 1989 and have treated over twenty thousand patients, I still feel that there is much to learn. I have used pressure points in martial art application thousands of times and believe that everyone can benefit from learning to use pressure points in self-defense and traditional martial art training. I also know that pressure points enhance any type of martial art technique whether it's self-defense, fighting, or training for good health. Pressure points can benefit all martial artists regardless of rank, system or style. I continue to study and learn about pressure points on a regular basis. I expect to continue with this interesting study for the rest of my life.

I moved to Houston, Texas in 1991, where I presently live with my family. I have dedicated my entire adult life to studying and practicing Korean martial arts. I have spent uncounted hours training my body and educating my mind. I truly believe that the martial arts, Kuk Sool in particular, have enriched and fulfilled my life in a way no other path could have.

As a small token of appreciation to my adopted culture that has given me ancient roots, and to the art that first introduced me to pressure points and Asian healing arts, I humbly decided to write this book.

There are those of us in search of
the Forgotten Knowledge,
while others search for
the Undiscovered Knowledge.
--R. Barry Harmon

POINT NUMBERS INDEX

This index lists the points by number, name and gives the page number they appear on.

Point Name & Number	Korean Name	Chinese Name	Japanese Name	Asian (Chinese) Character	Page Number
The Lung Channel					
Lung 1	Joong Boo	Zhong Fu	Chufu	中府	28
Lung 2	Oon Moon	Yun Men	Unmon	雲門	29
Lung 3	Chun Boo	Tian Fu	Tenpu	天府	30
Lung 5	Chuck Taek	Chi Ze	Shakutaku	尺澤	31
Lung 7	Yuhl Gyuhl	Lie Que	Rekketsu	列缺	32
The Large Intestine Channel					
Large Intestine 4	Hahp Gohk	He Gu	Gokoku	合谷	36
Large Intestine 5	Yang Gyea	Yang Xi	Yokei	陽谿	37
Large Intestine 10	Soo Sahm Nee	Shou San Li	Te no sanri	手三里	38
Large Intestine 11	Gohk Jee	Qu Chi	Kyokuchi	曲池	39

Point Name & Number	Korean Name	Chinese Name	Japanese Name	Asian (Chinese) Character	Page Number
Large Intestine 14	Bee Noe	Bi Nao	Hiju	臂臑	40
Large Intestine 16	Kuh Gohl	JuGu	Kokotsu	巨骨	41
Large Intestine 17	Chun Jung	Tian Ding	Tentei	天鼎	42
Large Intestine 18	Boo Dohl	Fu Tu	Hutotsu	扶突	43
Large Intestine 20	Young Hyang	Ying Xiang	Geiko	迎香	44
The Stomach Channel					
Stomach 1	Seung Eup:	Cheng Qi	Shokyu	承泣	47
Stomach 2	Sah Baek	Si Bai	Shihaku	四白	48
Stomach 4	Jee Chang	Di Cang	Chiso	地倉	49
Stomach 5	Dae Young	Da Ying	Daigei	大迎	50
Stomach 6	Hyup Guh	Jia Che	Kyosha	頰車	51
Stomach 7	Ha Gwan	Xia Guan	Gekan	下關	52
Stomach 9	In Young	Ren Ying	Jingei	人迎	53

Point Name & Number	Korean Name	Chinese Name	Japanese Name	Asian (Chinese) Character	Page Number
Stomach 10	Soo Dohl	Shui Tu	Suitotsu	水突	54
Stomach 11	Ki Sah	Qi She	Kisha	氣舍	55
Stomach 12	Kyuhl Boon	Que Pen	Ketsubon	缺盆	56
Stomach 18	You Guen	Ru Gen	Nyukon	乳根	57
Stomach 32	Bohk Toe	Fu Tu:	Fukuto	伏兔	58
Stomach 33	Umshi	Yinshi	Inshi	阴市	59
Stomach 35	Dohk Bee	Du Bi	Tokubi	犊鼻	60
Stomach 36	Johk Sahm Nee	Su San Li	Ashi no Sanri	足三里	61
Stomach 42	Choong Yang	Chong Yang	Shoyo	沖陽	62
Stomach 43	Hahm Gohk	Xiang Gu	Kankoku	陷谷	63
The Spleen Channel					
Spleen 6	Sahm Um Kyo	San Yin Jiao	Saninko	三陰交	66
Spleen 10	Hyul Hae	Xue Hai	Kekkai	血海	67
Spleen 12	Choong Moon	Chong Men	Shomon	沖門	68

Point Name & Number	Korean Name	Chinese Name	Japanese Name	Asian (Chinese) Character	Page Number
Spleen 21	Dae Po	Da Bao	Daiho	大包	69
The Heart Channel					
Heart 1	Geuk Chun	Ji Quan	Kyokusen	極泉	72
Heart 3	Soh Hae	Shao Hai	Shokai	少海	73
Heart 4	Young Doh	Ling Dao	Reido	靈道	74
Heart 5	Tong Ri	Tong Li	Tsuri	通里	75
Heart 6	Um Geuk	Yin Xi	Ingeki	陰郄	76
Heart 7	Shin Moon	Shen Men	Shinmon	神門	77
The Small Intestine Channel					
Small Intestine 8	Soh Hae	Xiao Hai	Shokai	小海	80
Small Intestine 9	Gyun Jung	Jian Zhen	Kentei	肩貞	81
Small Intestine 10	Noe Yoo	Nao Shu	Juyu	臑俞	82
Small Intestine 11	Chun Jong	Tian Zong	Tenso	天宗	83
Small Intestine 16	Chun Chang	Tian Chuang	Tenso	天窗	84

Point Name & Number	Korean Name	Chinese Name	Japanese Name	Asian (Chinese) Character	Page Number
Small Intestine 17	Chun Yong	Tian Rong	Tenyo	天容	85
The Urinary Bladder Channel					
Urinary Bladder 10	Chun Joo	Tian Zhu	Tenchu	天柱	88
Urinary Bladder 23	Shin Yoo	Shen Shu	Jinyu	腎俞	89
Urinary Bladder 39	Wee Yang	Wei Yang	Iyo	委陽	90
Urinary Bladder 40	Wee Joong	Wei Zhong	Ichu	委中	91
Urinary Bladder 42	Baek Ho	Po Hu	Hakko	魄戶	92
Urinary Bladder 44	Shin Dahng	Shen Tang	Shindo	神堂	93
Urinary Bladder 46	Kyuk Gwan	Ge Guan	Kakukan	膈關	94
Urinary Bladder 47	Hohn Moon	Hun Men	Konmon	魂門	95
Urinary Bladder 52	Jee Shil	Zhi Shi	Shishitsu	志室	96

Point Name & Number	Korean Name	Chinese Name	Japanese Name	Asian (Chinese) Character	Page Number
Urinary Bladder 57	Seung Sahn	Cheng Shan	Shozan	承山	97
Urinary Bladder 62	Shin Maek	Shen Mai	Shinmyaku	申脈	98
The Kidney Channel					
Kidney 1	Yong Chun	Yong Quan	Yusen	涌泉	101
Kidney 10	Um Gohk	Yin Gu	Inkoku	陰谷	103
The Pericardium Channel					
Pericardium 1	Chun Ji	Tian Chi	Tenchi	天池	106
Pericardium 3	Gohk Taek	Qu Ze	Kyokutaku	曲澤	107
Pericardium 6	Nae Gwan	Nei Guan	Naikan	內關	108
Pericardium 8	No Goong	Lao Gong	Rokyu	勞宮	109
The Triple Burner Channel					
Triple Burner 10	Chun Jung	Tian Jing	Tensei	天井	112
Triple Burner 17	Yea Poong	Yi Feng	Eifu	翳風	113
Triple Burner 20	Gahk Sohn	Jiao Sun	Kakuson	角孫	114

Point Name & Number	Korean Name	Chinese Name	Japanese Name	Asian (Chinese) Character	Page Number
The Gall Bladder Channel					
Gall Bladder 3	Gaek Joo In:	Shang Guan	Jyokan	上關	117
Gall Bladder 20	Poong Jee	Feng Chi	Fuchi	風池	119
Gall Bladder 21	Gyun Jung	Jian Jing	Kensei	肩井	120
Gall Bladder 25	Gyung Moon	Jing Men	Keimon	京門	121
Gall Bladder 26	Dae Make	Dai Mai	Taimyaku	帶脈	122
Gall Bladder 30	Hwan Doh	Huan Tiao	Kancho	環跳	123
Gall Bladder 31	Poong Shee	Feng Shi	Fushi	風市	124
Gall Bladder 32	Joong Dohk	Zhong Du	Chutoku	中瀆	125
Gall Bladder 34	Yang Neung Chun	Yang Ling Quan	Yoryosen	陽陵泉	126
The Liver Channel					
Liver 3	Tae Choong	Tai Chong	Taisho	太沖	129
Liver 9	Um Bo	Yin Bao	Impo	陰包	130

Point Name & Number	Korean Name	Chinese Name	Japanese Name	Asian (Chinese) Character	Page Number
Liver 13	Jang Moon	Zhang Men	Shomon	章門	131
Liver 14	Kee Moon	Qi Men	Kimon	期門	132
The Governing Channel					
Governing 4	Myung Moon	Ming Men	Meimon	命門	137
Governing 11	Shin Doh	Shen Dao	Shindo	神道	138
Governing 12	Shin Joo	Shen Zhu	Shinchu	身柱	139
Governing 14	Dae Cho	Da Zhui	Daitsui	大椎	140
Governing 15	Ah Moon	Ya Men	Amon	啞門	141
Governing 16	Poong Boo	Feng Fu	Fufu	風府	143
Governing 20	Baek Hae	Bai Hui	Hyakue	百會	144
Governing 24	Shin Jung	Shen Ting	Shintei	神庭	146
Governing 25	So Ryo	Su Liao	Soryo	素髎	147
Governing 26	In Joong	Shui Gou	Suiko	人中	148

Point Name & Number	Korean Name	Chinese Name	Japanese Name	Asian (Chinese) Character	Page Number
The Conception Channel					
Conception 2	Gok Gohl	Qu Gu	Kyokkotsu	曲骨	152
Conception 3	Joong Geuk	Zhong Ji	Chukyoku	中極	153
Conception 4	Gwan Won	Guan Yuan	Kangen	關元	154
Conception 5	Suhk Moon	Shi Men	Sekimon	石門	155
Conception 6	Ki Hae	Qi Hai	Kikai	氣海	156
Conception 7	Um Kyo	Yin Jiao	Inko	陰交	157
Conception 8	Shin Gwuhl	Shen Que	Shinketsu	神闕	158
Conception 9	Soo Boon	Shui Fen	Suibun	水分	159
Conception 10	Ha Wan	Xia Wan	Gekan	下脘	160
Conception 11	Kuhl Rhee	Jian Li	Kenri	建里	161
Conception 15	Goo Mee	Jiu Wei	Kyubi	鳩尾	162

Point Name & Number	Korean Name	Chinese Name	Japanese Name	Asian (Chinese) Character	Page Number
Conception 17	Dahn Joong	Dan Zhong	Danchu	膻中	163
Conception 22	Chun Dohl	Tian Tu	Tentotsu	天突	164
Conception 23	Yum Chun	Lian Quan	Rensen	廉泉	165

Extra Points and Striking Areas:

English Point / Area Name	Korean Name	Korean Character	Chinese & Japanese Character	Page Number
Temple	Dae Yang	대양	中文：太阳	167
Groin	Sah-Tah-Koo-Ni	사타구니	中文：腹股沟	168
Ear Drums	Kwee-Chung or Ko-Mahk	귀청: 고막	中文： 鼓膜	169
Eyes	Nuen	눈	中文： 目	170
Under the Tongue point	Hyuh Hyul	혀혈	中文: 舌	171
Under the Chin point	Ah-Gu Hyul	아구혈	中文： 上廉泉	172
Side of Neck Point	Hohn Soo Hyul	혼수혈	中文： 洪音穴	173

Total of 111 points listed including the extra points and striking areas:

BIBLIOGRAPHY

Bernard C. Kolster: *Pictorial Atlas of Acupuncture*: *An Illustrated manual* of *acupuncture points*. English Translation from German By: Colin Grant in association with Goodfellow and Egan: Ullmann publishing 2005.

Peter Deadman & Mazin Al-Khafaji with Kevin Baker: *A Manual of Acupuncture:* By the Journal of Chinese Medicine Publications: 2006.

Tyme: *Student Manual of the Fundamentals of Traditional Oriental Medicine:* Published by: Living Earth Enterprises 2001.

Zhou Mei-sheng; Translated by: Huang Shi & Zhang Zai-yi: *Explanation of Names of Acu-Points: With Its English Translation:* Anhui Publishing House of Science & Technology: 1985.

Nigel Wiseman, Andrew Ellis, Paul Zmiewski: *Fundamentals of Chinese Medicine:* Paradigm Publications 1985.

Shanghai College of Traditional Medicine 1974: *Acpuncture, A comprehensive Text:* Translated by, John O'Connor and Dan Bensky: Shanghai College of Traditional Medicine: Eastland Press 1981.

In Hyuk Suh: *Kuk Sool Won™ Textbook Volume 2:* Published by: World Kuk Sool Association 1993.

Seung, Cheong-woo: *Moxibustionnology:* Academy Publishing Company 1990.

Giovanni Maciocia: *The Foundations of Chinese Medicine: A comprehensive text for acupuncturists and herbalists:* Churchhill Livingstone, New York 1989

Bob Flaws: *Hit Medicine: Chinese Medicine In Injury Management:* Blue Poppy Press 1983

World Health Organization: *Standard Acupuncture Nomenclature: Second Edition:* World Health Organization Publications, 1993

Harriet Beinfield, L.Ac. and Efrem Korngold, L.Ac.O.M.D.: *Between Heaven and Earth, A Guide to Chinese Medicine:* Ballantine Books 1991

CPSIA information can be obtained
at www.ICGtesting.com
Printed in the USA
BVOW10s0613170316

440523BV00026B/200/P